Dear Rita:

My life-as-author has begun! Thank you not only for your kind endorsement, but your encouragement of my work. Blessings to you in your future writing and teaching. May we both find grace and bring much glory to God in all our endeavors.

Love,
Susan E. Erikson

When Dragons War

When Dragons War

A Confident Engagement Through Prayer,
Through Praise, and Through God's Word

By Susan Erikson

RESOURCE *Publications* · Eugene, Oregon

WHEN DRAGONS WAR
A Confident Engagement Through Prayer, Through Praise, and Through God's Word

Resource Publications
An Imprint of Wipf and Stock Publishers
199 W. 8th Ave., Suite 3
Eugene, OR 97401

www.wipfandstock.com

PAPERBACK ISBN: 978-1-5326-5811-2
HARDCOVER ISBN: 978-1-5326-5812-9
EBOOK ISBN: 978-1-5326-5813-6

Manufactured in the U.S.A.   09/20/18

Dedication

It is only before Christ that I can lay my burdens down. Only in his word do I find hope and strength in the midst of battle.

To God be the glory!

Contents

Permissions

Acknowledgments

I AM THANKFUL FOR my church family, who have prayed for me, and encouraged me. I am grateful for my pastor, Ted Hamilton, whose gospel-centered sermons continue to enrich my heart and my writing. I also want to thank the women of who have labored beside me in the word. I have been surrounded for years by women of prayer, women who love the word, and women who have graciously read and commented on my essays and poetry with kindness and honesty. I am indebted to them for their encouragement, and the depth of their biblical and compassionate wisdom. There are so many there isn't enough space to here to mention them all. Ladies: you know who you are, and you are much loved.

I am also thankful to Mary Weller, for being my first editor, and Michele Wagner for bringing the shine to its final editing.

I want to give special thanks to the following people:

First, I want to thank my father, Samuel Elder, who now enjoys God's presence face-to-face, for giving me from the very beginning, a love of Scripture, and the beautiful truth that life is intended to be spent in joyful worship of God. Secondly, I thank my mother, Sylvia Elder, for always being an attentive and instructive listening ear. Her comments have made me a better writer. Thirdly, I am thankful for my sisters (Sarah Elder, Kathy Volz, Lee Hethcox, Louise Chestnut, and Sharon Thayer) for graciously allowing me to share some of the family lore. Fourthly, I am thankful for my children and their spouses (Raymond and Juliana; David and Alicia; and Rebecca and Joe), for teaching me how to love with grace, with compassion, and with wisdom. Finally, I am thankful for my husband, Larry, for his love, his encouragement, and his prayers. To me a computer is a wondrous and magical typewriter with gifts unknown in my Smith-Corona days. I create. I write. To Larry, the computer is an amazing tool, and he is its master. He polishes, and makes beautiful copy. I couldn't manage without him. We are a great team, and I am very grateful.

Introduction

I HAVE THOUGHT A great deal about dragons lately. They appear in some form in every culture from the most primeval civilizations on into the modern age. In the myths of man, they have been revered, feared, worshiped, and conquered. I believe dragons are part of our most ancient memory; the battle in the Garden of Eden between Humankind and the Serpent. Thousands of years later we are still there, mesmerized by the Serpent's guile and seduction of our baser natures (hence the reverence and worship), yet we remain overwhelmed by the horrifying consequences of our own rebellion (fear and conquest). Dragons feed our egos, while destroying us in the process. We have been at war with ourselves, each other, and the universe since Genesis 3, and our only hope is the promise of a Warrior capable of conquering that which we both love and despise.

Because of your allegiance to Jesus Christ, you have been brought into that ancient conflict between the people of God, and the world of The Dragon. You and I live in the age of spiritual warfare, the age of dragons. You may have recently awakened to the fact that you are on the front lines. Or maybe you have been in the battle for a while; aware, yet struggling, and wondering how you are going to get through each day.

Only one slayer can truly save you and me, can truly conquer wayward hearts and crush the Serpent's head. Only His work ends the war. And paradoxically, this champion does not come with a great sword of power like Beowulf, or St. George, but as a willing sacrifice on a bloody cross. His blood is more powerful than any human weapon because death was required to conquer the dragon; the death of the Innocent One who never rebelled, for the sake of all of us who did. He lived like we never could, for we would always love the dragon more. He died as we never could, accepting the full wrath God intended for each of us. Then this slayer, the Christ, blew away death and walked out of a tomb. Christ's sacrifice breaks all our rules of engagement, and He continues to turn our world upside down.

So grab your gear, and come join me as we follow Christ right down into the midst of the battles that face us every day.

How Do I Read This Book?

This is your battle manual. For the next thirty-five weeks, you are going to explore the best weapons to use against dragons.

Recognize that not all the dragons in our lives are "out there." Some are in our own hearts, waiting to trip us up—our anger, our pride, our selfishness. These flaws are tools in The Dragon's hands to destroy us, but opportunities in Christ's hands to grow us, to conform us to his image, and give us the wisdom and strength to carry on. Weakness under the power and direction of God can be a powerful weapon against The Dragon and our temptations. Jesus Christ and his Gospel are your shields against the daily battles of this life.

Each weekly topic is divided into five daily readings to help you digest the material as you dig more deeply into your understanding of Christ and his Gospel.

Look for:

Studying the Battle Plan—Passages of Scripture that connect you to what the Word of God has to say on the subject at hand.

Scouting the Territory—Essays that further unpack the weekly Scripture readings.

Postings from the Front—Quotes from many who have been in the battle before you.

In The Trenches—Thought-provoking questions for each daily reading.

Heart Check—How can I apply what I've learned this week to real life?

Learn who God is, and who you are in Christ. Ask yourself: Where am I headed? If I look down I see myself and my weaknesses. If I look forward, I see whom I am following: the Christ who has saved and redeemed me, the Great Warrior who will preserve and sustain me to the end. If I look up, I just may see where I am headed home.

Dragon Thoughts

They asked the dragons in to eat with us.
Strange fellowship.
"Take their hands," they said,
"and talk with them.
But watch their claws.
They scratch."
They do indeed.

How can the two,
A dragon and a man,
Find fellowship and truce,
When one would eat the other
at a stroke?
What foolishness is this,
A cosmic joke,
That we could carry fire close to home,
And not expect
we would get burned?

The smoke is there already,
Rising high in tendriled steam,
A fog of misdirection,
Breath obscuring,
Covering up the truth unseen—
That dragons are still dragons
waiting patiently to eat,
And man is yet a man, most fragile,
Subtleties of grace to some and others, meat.

Allies

"So God created man in his own image, in the image of God he created him; male and female he created them" (Gen 1:27 ESV).

Week 1—Allies

Day 1

Studying the Battle Plan

"Then the LORD God said, 'It is not good that the man should be alone; I will make him a helper fit for him'. . . . So the LORD God caused a deep sleep to fall upon the man, and while he slept took one of his ribs and closed up its place with flesh. And the rib that the LORD God had taken from the man he made into a woman and brought her to the man. Then the man said, 'This at last is bone of my bones and flesh of my flesh; she shall be called Woman, because she was taken out of Man.' Therefore a man shall leave his father and his mother and hold fast to his wife, and they shall become one flesh. And the man and his wife were both naked and were not ashamed" (Gen 2:18, 21–25).

Postings from the Front

"Immediately upon creating Adam and Eve, God did something that he had not done with anything else he made. He spoke to them. This mundane moment was a moment of transcendence! The Lord, King, and Creator of the universe was speaking the secrets of his divine wisdom into the ears of the people he had made. In this act God was calling Adam and Eve to transcend the boundaries of their own thoughts, interpretations, and experiences. They were to form their lives by the origin-to-destiny perspective that only the Creator could have . . . By themselves they never could have discovered the things he told them . . . These treasures of wisdom would only be known by Adam and Eve because God decided to reveal them . . . Never were Adam and Eve built to exist on conclusions drawn from their experience, or concepts resulting from autonomous interpretations. Every thought was meant to be shaped by the truth glory that he would patiently and progressively impart to them."—Paul David Tripp[1]

In The Trenches

1. What does verse 18 ("Then the LORD God said, 'It is not good that the man should be alone; I will make him a helper fit for him.'") tell us about the character of God? What does it tell us about Adam and Eve's relationship to God?

2. Genesis 1:27 tells us that, "God created man in his own image, in the image of God he created them, male and female he created them." To be created in the image of God is to be God's representative, to rule the earth under God's authority. It also means that human beings are different than all other creatures in God's world. Human beings resemble God in that we think, talk, make decisions, and make choices. We remember what has already happened, and we tell stories. We write our stories down so that we can continue to remember. And we have the ability to create things like paintings, sculpture, and music, as well as conduct science experiments, and solve math problems. When God says he made us male and female, he is also telling us that we are supposed to make families and communities. We each have jobs to do. What do verses 15 ("The LORD God took the man and put him in the garden of Eden to work it and keep it") and 19 ("Now out of the ground the LORD God had formed every beast of the field and every bird of the heavens and brought them to the man to see what he would call them") tell us about Adam's job and his position in the garden?

Day 2

Scouting the Territory

My niece is getting married this afternoon, and there has been a flurry of activity the past few weeks: extensive house cleaning and touch-up

1. Tripp, *A Quest for More*, 19.

painting, last minute checks on guest lists, manicures and pedicures, and new clothes for everyone. The bride and all of her attendants are getting their hair professionally done this morning, all in anticipation of the Big Event, a grand celebration of ceremony and feasting later today.

Today's passage is about the very first wedding. Instead of relatives, the animals were gathered around the groom so that he could name them; identify them by species, by group; exercising his job as caretaker of creation. In the process of categorizing two cats, two giraffes, and two elephants, he realized there was only one Adam. The groom needed a bride. God wanted his caretaker to recognize this, hence the constant parade of two–by–twos before the one man.

The first wedding preparations didn't include mani–pedis, new paint, or new clothes, but a new surgery; the removal of a portion of the man to make a woman. Even the names in Hebrew hint at this. "Man," *ish*, and "woman," *ishshah*, show how much one is part of the other. The surgery was followed by celebration as the groom exclaimed, "This at last is bone of my bones and flesh of my flesh; she shall be called Woman because she was taken out of Man" (Gen 2:23). "She is part of me," he is saying with masculine awe, looking at his lovely bride. "She is perfect!" Isn't that what we hear newlyweds say when they glowingly promise the world and themselves to each other while exchanging rings? If being perfect for each other was all it took to make a marriage, we could stop right here and let the pink haze of infatuation surrounding this happy couple slowly fade them out of the picture. But we, like them, need perspective, and only God can properly define this relationship.

And so the ceremony begins: "Therefore, a man shall leave his father and his mother and hold fast to his wife, and they shall become one flesh" (Gen 2:24). "Hold fast," God says. That is the language of covenant faithfulness. Not just between husband and wife, but, God says, also between the couple and God. In much later years, the prophet, Malachi, rebukes Israel's disregard for marriage with these words, "But you say, 'Why does he not [accept the people's offerings]?' Because the LORD was witness between you and the wife of your youth, to whom you have been faithless, though she is your companion and your wife by covenant. Did he not make them one, with a portion of the Spirit in their union?" (Mal 2:14–15a) Even Adam's words, "bone of my bones," expresses covenant language according to the ESV study notes, "where Adam commits himself to Eve before God by employing a formula which is attested elsewhere in covenant–ratifying contexts."[2]

So much for that pink haze of infatuation. It may not last past the first slice of cake. Yet a marriage is meant to be an alliance that lasts a lifetime. Scripture is telling us that it is less about that wonderful, warm feeling, the fabulous dress, and the romantic candles; and more about a lifelong, God–centered commitment between the *ish* and the *ishshah*. Like having signed a contract, the husband and the wife have declared to be accountable before God and each other as long as they live. This is not the romantic, fuzzy feelings of a novel, but the clear–headed romance of faithfulness, of friendship and delight in two people that know they are going to stick it out no matter what, and always be there for each other.

In The Trenches

1. When you play on a softball team, is everyone a shortstop? What does it mean to be part of a team?

2. Genesis 2:20 says that Adam needed "a helper fit for him." The Hebrew word for helper is *ezer*. The ESV Study Bible notes tell us that the *ezer* is the "one who supplies strength in the area that is lacking in 'the helped.'"[3] That means that Adam didn't have the ability to do everything all by himself. Some things he did better than Eve. Some things Eve did better than Adam. Together they could do the best job. Adam needed an Eve to help him do his job. They were meant to be a team. How did Adam discover he needed a helper? Why do you think it was so important for Adam to realize he needed Eve and not have God just tell him?

Day 3

Scouting the Territory

You have been looking for dragons and not finding them. There is a good reason. Dragons are intruders. They do not belong. God created his world to be a beautiful place, where he could be in perfect fellowship with the

2. ESV study notes, 1776.

3. ESV study notes, 54.

man and the woman he made, and the man and the woman would have perfect fellowship with each other. Beware. Be watchful. We haven't gotten there yet, but we will soon discover that our first parents will actually invite their worst enemy, The Dragon, right into their holy garden! "But dragons are dangerous!" you say. I agree. Adam and Eve don't know that yet. They are not expecting The Dragon to be waiting in the shadows, preparing to destroy their beautiful alliance.

Even today, I don't think the loving newlyweds I have witnessed really believe while they are standing up before God and witnesses, that there are dragons waiting for them as well; dragons within and without, anything to keep "this man" and "this woman" apart. Forty–four years ago, I certainly wasn't entertaining such thoughts while promising to love, honor, and obey. It didn't match the picture of the beautiful wedding, or my handsome new husband.

But God knew. That's why he laid out the framework for the husband and wife—leave your father and mother, hold fast to each other. Become one flesh. Be faithful to me, says God, and to each other. A tall order, considering The Dragon in waiting will encourage the birth of a whole host of dragonish ways. That's why God sent his Son to reconcile people who aren't aware yet that they may one day despise each other, be so angry with each other that they would refuse to talk with one another, refuse to stay in the same room. Some days only the cross stands between a couple and their dragons.

In The Trenches

1. A covenant is a solemn contract between two or more people. Both sides agree to obey the rules and help each other no matter what. A marriage is a type of covenant. What covenant did God command Adam and Eve, as well as every married couple, to follow?

2. God intended the marriage covenant to be between one man and one woman. This is so important that God told Timothy in the New Testament that a man who was a leader in the church must be married to only one woman. Read 1 Timothy 3:2–5. What kind of man makes a good leader? Why do these character traits make a difference in his marriage?

Day 4

Studying the Battle Plan

"Be filled with the Spirit, addressing one another in psalms and hymns and spiritual songs, singing and making melody to the Lord with your heart, giving thanks always and for everything to God the Father in the name of our Lord Jesus Christ, submitting to one another out of reverence for Christ. Wives, submit to your own husbands, as to the Lord. For the husband is the head of the wife even as Christ is the head of the church, his body, and is himself its Savior. Now as the church submits to Christ, so also wives should submit in everything to their husbands. Husbands, love your wives, as Christ loved the church and gave himself up for her, that he might sanctify her, having cleansed her by the washing of water with the word, so that he might present the church to himself in splendor, without spot or wrinkle or any such thing, that she might be holy and without blemish. In the same way husbands should love their wives as their own bodies. He who loves his wife loves himself. For no one ever hated his own flesh, but nourishes and cherishes it, just as Christ does the church, because we are members of his body. 'Therefore a man shall leave his father and mother and hold fast to his wife, and the two shall become one flesh.' This mystery is profound, and I am saying that it refers to Christ and the church. However, let each one of you love his wife as himself, and let the wife see that she respects her husband" (Eph 5:18b–33).

Jesus says, "So they are no longer two but one flesh. What therefore God has joined together, let not man separate" (Matt 19:6). How can we daily keep from separating ourselves from each other? We must put on Christ and let him rule our willful and dragonish hearts. "Submit to one another out of reverence for Christ," says Paul in Ephesians 5:21. "Put on then, as God's chosen ones, holy and beloved, compassionate hearts, kindness, humility, meekness, and patience, bearing with one another," continues Paul in Colossians. "And, if one has a complaint against another, forgiving each other, as the Lord has forgiven you, so you also must forgive. And above all these put on love, which binds everything together in perfect harmony. And let the peace of Christ rule in your hearts, to which indeed you were called in one body. And be thankful" (Col 3:12–15). Beware of dragons. Cling to Christ. Walk together. Hold fast. And the alliance begins.

In The Trenches

1. The Bible tells us the best way to understand the Bible! If you are not sure what a passage means, look for other passages in the Bible on the subject. Ephesians 5:21 helps us understand Genesis 2. How were Adam and Eve meant to be a team?

2. This passage also tells us that marriage is one of God's pictures to explain to us what his relationship with his people is meant to look like. God even calls his people his "bride" in many places throughout Scripture. What does marriage tell us about God's relationship with us? What does it tell us about our relationship with God? What does it tell us about how we are to live in a marriage if we love God?

3. Because we are sinners, even Christian married people often do not work as a team. Because we are fighting our dragon hearts, we fail. What does Scripture tell us to do?

Day 5

Heart Check

The Westminster Confession of Faith reminds us that the chief end of man is to glorify God and enjoy him forever. What better weapon against dragons than to take the focus off ourselves, and actively focus on our Savior!

"Therefore, as you received Christ Jesus the Lord, so walk in him, rooted and built up in him and established in the faith, just as you were taught, abounding in thanksgiving" (Col 2:6).

Consider memorizing this verse. Take it to heart. Can you name five things you can thank God for?

War

"Sin is crouching at the door. Its desire is contrary to you, but you must rule over it" (Gen 4:7b).

Week 2—Changing Allies

Day 1

Studying the Battle Plan

"Now the serpent was more crafty than any other beast of the field that the LORD God had made. He said to the woman, 'Did God actually say, "You shall not eat of any tree in the garden"?' And the woman said to the serpent, 'We may eat of the fruit of the trees in the garden, but God said, "You shall not eat of the fruit of the tree that is in the midst of the garden, neither shall you touch it, lest you die."' But the serpent said to the woman, 'You shall not die. For God knows that when you eat of it your eyes will be opened, and you will be like God, knowing good and evil.' So when the woman saw that the tree was good for food, and that it was a delight to the eyes, and that the tree was to be desired to make one wise, she took of its fruit and ate, and she also gave some to her husband who was with her, and he ate. Then the eyes of both were opened, and they knew that they were naked. And they sewed fig leaves together and made themselves loincloths" (Gen 3:1–7).

In The Trenches

1. Here is the beginning of sin in human history. Do you notice how Eve and the serpent are talking to each other? Are they each telling the truth?

2. Why do you think the serpent talked to Eve and not to Adam? He had to be nearby to take the fruit offered to him.

Day 2

Scouting the Territory

> *Arom*–to be naked. In the context of Genesis 2:25 implies inno-
> cence, honesty, nothing hidden.
>
> *Arum*–to be crafty, shrewd.
>
> *Erom*–to be naked, but the sense of innocence was gone.
>
> Deut. 28:48 unpacks the meaning best–it is nakedness under
> God's judgment.[1]

Arom, arum, and erom[2]–three Hebrew words that are a Genesis pun to describe a world turned upside down. *Arom* means "naked." "And the man
and his wife were both naked [*arom*] and were not ashamed" (Gen 2:25).
They were naked and innocent, open and transparent, and without guile.
Then the next sentence is abrupt. "Now the serpent was more crafty [*arum*,
meaning shrewd], than any other beast of the field that the LORD God had
made" (Gen 3:1a). Innocence is about to be ripped inside out by shrewd
deception.

"Did God actually say?"

God's commands, says the serpent, are open for discussion and interpretation. "You shall not eat of any tree in the garden" (Gen 3:1b). This
is what is called a "straw man" argument. It's not true. It sounds enough
like what is true to be glossed over. And it changes the whole context. Of
course God didn't say all the trees were off limits. He specified just one. But
now the thought is hanging in the air: he is keeping you from something
you want. Not that he has given you everything, but that he is withholding
something, something important. And Eve is only too willing to add to
her adversary's argument–"neither shall you touch it" (Gen 3:3). Dragon
smoke, like obscuring fog is circling the couple. "Now what did he say?" Eve
is thinking, trying to keep the facts straight. But the yearning for something
untouchable is clawing at her heart and mind.

---

1. Sailhamer, Genesis, 84. I am indebted to the work of John Sailhamer on his use of
these Hebrew terms.

2. Sailhamer, Ibid., 84.

The serpent comes in for the kill. "For God knows that when you eat of it your eyes will be opened, and you will be like God, knowing good and evil" (Gen 3:5).

I not only want this, think Adam and Eve, but I need it. There was that passing comment from God, "lest you die," that should have set off warning bells, but two hearts have been opened to accept a terrible possibility. And the deed is done. *Arom* has been chewed up and spit out by *arum*; the juice of the fruit already "a horrid stain"[3] around both eager mouths. Here lies the appalling pun. *Arum* has taken the meaning of duplicity, and attached itself to nakedness. Now nakedness in this world will have the whiff of deception and betrayal.

C. S. Lewis explains it so clearly in *The Magician's Nephew*: "That is what happens to those who pluck and eat fruits at the wrong time and in the wrong way. The fruit is good, but they loathe it ever after."[4] This loathing is not only of the tree or its fruit, but of self, which gnaws and rips apart the relationship between the man and the woman, and cuts off the connection with the Creator. And because of this, nakedness is no longer a joy but a terror. The third Hebrew pun, *erom*, which also means naked, now describes God's beautiful creation gone awry. "Then the eyes of both were opened, and they knew that they were naked [*erom*]" (Gen 3:7). John Sailhamer (Professor of Old Testament at Golden Gate Baptist Theological Seminary, Berea, California), in his commentary on Genesis states, "The effect of the fall is not simply that the man and the woman become aware of their 'nakedness' (*arom*). Rather, they come to know that they are 'naked' (*erom*) in the sense of being 'under God's judgment.'"[5] Trust is gone. Only covering, hiding, and blaming remain. "In the Bible," writes Bruce Waltke (Professor of Old Testament at Reformed Theological Seminary, Orlando, Florida), "*arum* usually describes someone stripped of protective clothing and 'naked' in the sense of being defenseless, weak, or humiliated."[6] This is the language of shame. Trusting God would have given them everything that is good. The man and the woman chose that day to trust in themselves, to decide for themselves what is right and good, and to this day, it has never given us anything of value. It has always destroyed.

One dragon stood at the entrance to Eden. Two more walked out.

3. Lewis, *The Magician's Nephew*, 174.

4. Lewis, Ibid., 190.

5. Sailhamer, Genesis, 84.

6. Waltke, Genesis, 92.

In The Trenches

1. Pride is all about me: my status, my superiority over others, my feelings about my own worth and value. The Bible already told us that God gave us enormous value when he made us in his image. Pride says that God's gifts are not enough! I decide what makes me special and valuable. Pride wants me to be God. Do you see pride in Adam and Eve?

2. What happened to Adam and Eve's relationship?

3. What happened to the man and woman in their relationship to God?

4. How does the Bible describe a dragon heart?

Day 3

Falling

She thought
to Know
Would grow divine,
Would make her light,
Would elevate
her power and right.

She,
Meant to be
the complement to Holy Kings,
the Other in God's sacred place.
Instead,
She desired to Know.

It made her petty,
Shrill,
It grew her inward,
Self-absorbed,
It gave her weight like lead
To Know

the ache of pain,
To Know
deep disappointment
mortaring a stony breast,
To Know
the gray without the good,
To Know,
To Know,
To Know too much,
To not regain
The simple peace,
The quiet thought,
The gentle space,
Now all displaced
by attitude,
by cringing shame,
Recriminations
closing down a shuttered soul.

Too hard to breathe,
Too cold for sighs.
Where can reprieve
unbind the lies
that ego craves?
Untangle
bites that knowledge gave?

In The Trenches

1. When is knowledge helpful? When is it destructive?
2. How do we know that Adam and Eve have become dragons?

Day 4

Postings from the Front

"The possibility of evil exists from the moment that a creature is made that can love and do good because it chooses and not because it is unable to do anything else. The actuality of evil exists from the moment that that choice is exercised in the wrong direction. Sin (moral evil) is the deliberate choice of the not–God. And pride, as the Church has consistently pointed out, is the root of it; i.e., the refusal to accept the creaturely status; the making of the difference between self and God into an antagonism against God. Satan, as Milton rightly shows, 'thinks himself impaired,' and in that moment he chooses that evil shall be his good."—Dorothy Sayers.[7]

"Fairy tales do not give the child his first idea of bogey. What fairy tales give the child is his first clear idea of the possible defeat of bogey. The baby has known the dragon intimately ever since he had an imagination. What the fairy tale provides for him is a St. George to kill the dragon." —G.K. Chesterton.

In The Trenches

1. What does it mean to choose "not–God?" Do you know when you are choosing "not–God?"
2. Read Romans 3:10–12. What does God say about us?

Day 5

Heart Check

"We have all become like one who is unclean, and all our righteous deeds are like a polluted garment. We all fade like a leaf, and our iniquities, like the wind, take us away" (Isa 64:6).

Do you recognize the dragon in you?

7. Sayers, *Letters to a Diminished Church*, 167.

Week 3—The Blame Game

Day 1

Studying the Battle Plan

"And they heard the sound of the LORD God walking in the garden in the cool of the day, and the man and his wife hid themselves from the presence of the LORD God among the trees of the garden. But the LORD God called to the man and said to him, 'Where are you?' And he said, 'I heard the sound of you in the garden, and I was afraid, because I was naked, and I hid myself.' He said, 'Who told you that you were naked? Have you eaten of the tree of which I commanded you not to eat?' The man said, 'The woman whom you gave to be with me, she gave me fruit of the tree, and I ate.' Then the LORD God said to the woman, 'What is this that you have done?' The woman said, 'The serpent deceived me, and I ate'" (Gen 3:8–13).

In The Trenches

1. How did the man and the woman respond to God when he came to talk with them? Why?

2. How did the man and woman respond to each other?

Day 2

Scouting the Territory

I am the oldest of five girls. When I was about ten years old, I hit upon the perfect solution for one of my most hated chores—changing the bed sheets. I would smooth the sheets and covers to make them look like they had been changed, and then crumple and stomp all over the clean sheets to make them look dirty, tossing what was clean into the dirty clothes hamper. I am not sure how long I got away with this ridiculous maneuver. My bedding must have been filthy!

One day my sister Sheila, two years younger, caught me in the act. Now there were two conspirators. Only she didn't even bother to unfold the clean sheets, but tossed them fresh and folded directly into the waiting hamper. Of course my mother noticed, and confronted Sheila, who immediately pointed to me. "Susan told me to do it." Now here is where my sinful heart was truly exposed. I lied. I looked properly appalled, and denied knowing anything about it. Sheila got into trouble. I didn't. Sheila never let me forget this as long as she lived. She is with Jesus now and no longer worried by such childish idiocy, and the rest of us all laugh, remembering this story as one of the many funny incidents in our family history. But our laughter is rueful. The funniest stories we tell about each other usually revolve around our shortcomings. We are truly daughters of Adam and Eve; hiding and lying, afraid to be found out, and looking for someone else to blame.

Being found out must have been a confusing and terrifying experience for our first parents, who had previously enjoyed perfect communion with God. Guilt and shame were new and uncomfortable feelings. Not so for us. We are, unfortunately, far too comfortable with the feelings. They have dogged us from our earliest memories. Adam and Eve didn't yet know that their rescue was possible. A few verses later they would hear, tucked within the lines of sin's sorry consequences, an expectation of hope—an offspring of the woman would one day rise up and smash the dragons that had suddenly grown between them and God.

Like my forbearers, I didn't realize back then how much God knew I would need a rescuer and had planned for just that contingency. I do now. Christ, the great Dragon Slayer, *did* come, and he continues to rescue sinful and foolish people like Sheila and me. Making my bed look changed and roughing up clean sheets was a lot more work and trouble than just changing the bed. I knew it was wrong. I didn't plan on getting caught. I was willing to let Sheila suffer for my sin. How thankful I am to know that Christ chose to suffer for my sins instead, to cover my foolishness and hers, with his love and grace.

Sheila died at the age of forty-four after a five year battle with cancer. It was a long goodbye, as cancer often is. But it was a farewell from the struggles and failures of this life into the hope and glory of heaven. All because the Son of God lived the life Sheila and I couldn't, and willingly took our blame on himself. Then he offered both of us his perfect record. I am grateful every day. And Sheila, having run her race with endurance, grabbed onto Christ with both hands, and joined the cloud of witnesses. No more blame. No more shame. No more dirty sheets. No more "What is this that you have done?" But lives lived on what Christ has done for us. And with that thought in mind, the whole silly incident makes me smile.

In The Trenches

1. Guilt is knowing we have done something wrong that needs to be fixed. How did I, as a child, try to fix my sheet problem? Did it make the situation better or worse?

   Shame is knowing we have done something wrong, and it affects how we feel about ourselves. We are a failure, and we can't fix it. What can feelings of shame do to our relationships with others?

2. The truth is that the guilt and shame that comes from our own sin is intended to tell us something. We have done something wrong, and we can't fix it. Both shame and guilt should lead us to Christ, the only one who can fix our problem with sin. Read Ephesians 2:1–9. What has Christ done for us? What comfort do we have in Christ?

Day 3

Postings from the Front

"First of all, it came over him like a thunder–clap that he had been running on all fours—and why on earth had he been doing that? And secondly, as he bent toward the water, he thought for a second that yet another dragon was staring up at him out of the pool. But in an instant he realized the truth. The dragon face in the pool was his own reflection. There was no doubt of it. It moved as he moved: it opened and shut its mouth as he opened and shut his. He had turned into a dragon while he was asleep. Sleeping on a dragon's hoard with greedy, dragonish thoughts in his heart, he had become a dragon himself."–C.S. Lewis.[1]

Awakenings

I ride!
I flee!
I cannot see what lies beneath.

Deny!
Deny!
Let rumors fly and carry me away
to safer,
kinder shores
where love is love is love is love.

But still I hear,
I hear myself,
My whisperings—"My loves, my choices, I decide,"
The demigods of fire rise up
higher, higher, ever higher,
Speaking,
Seething restless smoke of my desire,
So I ride.

I cannot flee!
I comprehend.
At last I see!

Dear heart,
The wars I fight are not outside.
They are in me.
I see what lies beneath!

---

1. Lewis, *Dawn Treader*, 91.

Dear God! Save me!
I am the dragon!
I am he.

I am the dragon!

In The Trenches

1. C.S. Lewis's book, *The Voyage of the Dawn Treader*, describes the experience of Eustace discovering he has become a dragon. Eustace, from our world, is on a Narnian adventure, traveling aboard King Caspian's ship as it goes from island to island. Eustace has discovered a dragon's hoard of gold. What made Eustace into a dragon?

2. *Awakenings* is a poem. A poem is a different way of explaining an experience. It uses metaphors and similes in short sentences to create an emotional experience. A simile says, "I am like a dragon." A metaphor says, "I am a dragon." In each case, the person has not, like Eustace, actually become a dragon. But the poem reminds us that we can have dragonish thoughts and do dragonish things. Read the poem aloud. What is the speaker trying to do in the poem?

3. What does it do to our behavior when we become a dragon in our thoughts?

4. How does the poem help us better understand how Eustace must have felt?

Day 4

Postings from the Front

"The Devil is a spiritual lunatic, but, like many lunatics, he is extremely plausible and cunning. His brain is, so to speak, in perfectly good working order except for that soft and corrupted spot in the center, where dwells the eternal illusion. His method of working is to present us with the magnificent setup, hoping we shall not use either our brains or our spiritual faculties to penetrate the illusion. He is playing for sympathy; therefore he is much better served by exploiting our virtues than by appealing to our lower passions; consequently, it is when the Devil looks most noble and reasonable that he is most dangerous."—Dorothy Sayers.[2]

In The Trenches

Dorothy Sayers is saying something very interesting about dragons: they love feelings, particularly if we make decisions *strictly* on our feelings. God gave us emotions to enjoy his world. We are in awe of a brilliant and multi-colored sunset, or filled with tears of joy at the birth of a baby. We feel great compassion for someone who is hurting, or anger at injustice. These are good things. But God commanded us to love him with all our heart, our soul, and our *mind* (Matt.22:37). Love always connects feelings to thinking, and directs our thoughts and our feelings toward God's truth. Satan just asks, "How does this make you feel?" God commands, "I have told you what is right. Now, how should you think about it, and what should you do?"

I didn't feel like changing my bed, so I didn't. It was too much work. My mother asked too much of me. She was forcing me to work too hard. I didn't need to do it. Besides, I had come up with the coolest way to beat the system. Isn't that what life is all about: "beating the system?" The legal courts would call it "premeditated," meaning planned. I intended to commit a crime. That day, I was a dragon: full of selfish, useless, feelings.

At the simplest level, I slept in a dirty, smelly bed. But it didn't stop there. I showed dishonor to my mother by not obeying her. When I didn't obey my mother, I also disobeyed God. I lied to my mother. I got my sister involved in my crime. I caused her to sin. My little rebellion of feelings turned into a huge offence against God, my mother, and my sister; all because I "didn't feel like it." Feelings without love or thought put me in a spiritually dangerous position. No wonder dragons love them!

1. Read Isaiah 26:3-4. How important is our mind?

2. Read Romans 12:2; Philippians 4:8-9; Colossians 3:1-4. Of what value is a mind and heart tuned to Christ, instead of only feelings?

---

2. Sayers, *Letters to a Diminished Church,* 169.

Day 5

Heart Check

1. Read Psalm 139:23–24. How easily we choose the dragon way! What does the psalmist ask of God as a remedy?

2. How easy it is to fail and be so totally blind to our own sin! Now read Psalm 139: 7–12. When I was a child I would read this passage and the little Sunday school song would pop into my head: "you cannot hide from God whatever you do, wherever you go." I thought I could hide my sin from my mother, but these verses said I couldn't hide my sin from God. This is true. God sees everything. He knows my heart. But as I have gotten older, I now realize the same verses carry a promise of great hope. When I feel lost, I know there is nowhere I can go where God cannot find me and rescue me. I need redemption every day. I need the healing that only he can bring.

3. Read 1 John 1:9, 4:4. God is greater than The Dragon, and God is ready and able to forgive us and completely take away our sin from us. Consider memorizing these two verses, and meditating on them.

Week 4—Our Imperfect Rule

Day 1

Studying the Battle Plan

"The LORD God said to the serpent, 'Because you have done this, cursed are you above all livestock and above all beasts of the field; on your belly you shall go, and dust you shall eat all the days of your life. I will put enmity between you and the woman, and between your offspring and her offspring; he shall bruise your head, and you shall bruise his heel.' To the woman he said, 'I will surely multiply your pain in childbearing; in pain you shall bring forth children. Your desire shall be for your husband, and he shall rule over you.' And to Adam he said, 'Because you have listened to the voice of your wife and have eaten of the tree of which I commanded you, "You shall not eat of it," cursed is the ground because of you; in pain you shall eat of it all the days of your life; thorns and thistles it shall bring forth for you; and you shall eat the plants of the field. By the sweat of your face you shall eat bread, till you return to the ground, for out of it you were taken; for you are dust, and to dust you shall return'" (Gen 3:14–19).

In The Trenches

1. Adam and Eve's rebellion against God affects every area of their lives. The man's calling is to provide for and protect his family, his team, from the outside world. What will happen to Adam?

The woman's calling is to carry and take care of children, and protect the inside world of their team. What will happen to Eve? What has happened to their team relationship?

2. Years later, in Exodus 34:6–7 God reveals himself to his people—"The LORD, the LORD, a God merciful and gracious, slow to anger, and abounding steadfast love and faithfulness, keeping steadfast love for thousands, forgiving iniquity and transgression and sin, but who will by no means clear the guilty, visiting the iniquity of the fathers on the children and the children's children, to the third and fourth generation." God has shown that there are consequences to Adam and Eve's sinful actions that affect not only them but all future generations. But he also shows his love and mercy to these two first people and to us. God has promised a rescue! Can you find it? What does he promise?

Day 2

Scouting the Territory

I have a golden retriever/yellow lab mix named Fitz. Today I had to have him put down. Fitz was a great friend for over eleven years; attentive, protective, gentle with children, and eager for a good walk. He was an animal companion in the best sense of the word. In the last few years of his life he developed a bad back, and was clearly going blind. A few days ago he couldn't get up off the floor. His legs and back were finally giving out. We forget that our sin affects all creation, not just a guarantee of weeds in the garden, pain in childbirth, and corrupted relationships. Animals get sick and old too. They suffer the pains and limitations brought on the earth by our sin. They die. And all creation, writes Paul in Romans 8:20–25, longs for the day when our salvation will finally be completed. Creation itself is not what it should be; subjected by God to frustration and futility due to human sin. The whole creation has been "groaning together in the pains of childbirth" (Rom 8:22) ever since.

Meanwhile, we, the broken kings and queens intended to rule over and protect God's world, are still his world's stewards. I am not like God. I am much more like Adam and Eve after the fall; very aware of my weaknesses, my insecurities, and weighted by my responsibilities. I am an imperfect guardian, called to speak and choose for Fitz. Today I do not like my job.

To show him kindness means to let him go, and I long for a better creation. Paul reminds me that the suffering of all creation, the suffering and death of Fitz, and someday of me, has within it a great hope. Just as the work of Christ has transformed me from lost sinner to redeemed child, there is also certainty in the resurrection of Christ of a greater future, a promise of final deliverance; the redemption of my body. As men and women, the caretakers of creation, will someday be set free from sin, creation itself will be changed. In the new heavens and earth, animals will be set free from their bondage in this fallen world to our corruption. Dogs are not us. But if there are dogs in the new earth, they will thrive in the life and health that God intends for them.

Paul says we and creation groan inwardly, but also wait eagerly. That is just how I feel today. Sin's futility swept over Fitz and me. But I will wait. With the Spirit's help, I will wait with patience. There is joy yet to come, and a certain and final end to a cycle of rebellion and destruction started so long ago.

In The Trenches

1. Have you ever had a dog or cat who was your best friend? And they died? Read Romans 8:19–25. The Apostle Paul tells us that all of creation suffers because of man's sin. Adam and Eve brought death into the world, and now our pet friends suffer and die as well. What will the work of Christ, the Dragon Slayer, mean to creation? What hope does creation long for?

2. What is our hope?

Day 3

In Memory of a Friend

When Adam sinned,
The fear of man crept in
to turn the beasts away.
No more the friend of princes,
Lions slunk off into shadows,
Elephants refused to play,

But dogs remained.

These dogs—
Face readers,
Companions for community,
Not just for work and hunt,
But for a friendship once displayed
before the Fall.
(When man,
The king,
And all the creatures he had named,
Enjoyed connections.)—
These dogs stayed.

Now all created beings feel the sting,
The alienation,
Lost and frayed by human will.
They know death.
But still are dogs.
They stay.

The dogs remain
a promise to this fallen prince,
That lion, lamb, and dog one day
will come to peace.
That enmity someday will end,
And earth no longer feel man's curse,
When man is freed eternally,
When all creation rises, fresh and new,
All recreated by Creator's Word,
And he intended to be regent will regain his seat
by Him who breathed this man from dust,
and gave him life.
Then all will breathe,
Alive,
And fears and old hostilities will cease.

In The Trenches

1. The poem, *In Memory of a Friend,* talks about dogs. What makes your pet special to you?

2. God created dogs to be unique creatures. They "read" faces. That means they can tell if you are sad or happy. They also follow your face, looking for direction. They are waiting for you to tell them what to do. Cats don't do that. Even monkeys and apes, who look more like us, can't do that. Dogs also like to be part of the "pack," the family group. How are we similar? How does having a relationship with a dog remind you of the world before sin?

Day 4

Read Psalm 104. It is a long psalm, but a wonderful praise picture of God and his creation.

In The Trenches

1. Does God take care of the animals? How do we know this?

2. How are we to respond?

Day 5

Heart Check

Consider reading all of Psalm 32. It is not just about asking God to forgive sin, but the realization that he has forgiven, the knowledge that his love surrounds us, that he brings deliverance. Those who do not know him stay in their sorrows. There is no one to lift their burdens away. True sorrow for our sin ends in forgiveness and should lead us to a heart of thanksgiving and praise. What a glorious gift from God!

Week 5—The Face of Death

Day 1

Studying the Battle Plan

"In the course of time Cain brought to the LORD an offering of the fruit of the ground, and Abel also brought of the firstborn of the flock and their fat portions. And the LORD had regard for Abel and his offering, but for Cain and his offering he had no regard. So Cain was very angry, and his face fell. The LORD said to Cain, 'Why are you angry, and why has your face fallen? If you do well, will you not be accepted? And if you do not do well, sin is crouching at the door. Its desire is contrary to you, but you must rule over it.' Cain spoke to Abel his brother. And when they were in the field, Cain rose up against his brother Abel and killed him" (Gen 4:3–8).

In The Trenches

1. Read Hebrews 11:4. How does this passage help explain the difference between Abel's and Cain's sacrifices? What or who was Abel trusting in?

2. Did Cain recognize his own dragon heart?

Day 2

Scouting the Territory

Sin has entered the world, yet Adam and Eve have been given a great hope. A child will come from them mighty enough to overcome the serpent. The dragon can yet be slain. Soon there are two boys. Is it Cain? Will it be Abel? And it is here that the true horror of what Adam and Eve have unleashed is made profoundly clear. Sin does not only make relationships awkward, or loaded with misunderstandings. Sin does not just make siblings into rivals. Sin destroys.

We who are so accustomed to the idea of murder, our sensibilities deadened by years of the evening news and the murder mystery genre, cannot quite comprehend the enormous wave of horror, guilt, shame and pain that must have washed over our first parents.

Where is the promise now? One bite, one selfish choice, has uncovered what already existed since the fall, waiting to be released. Sin is not just about minor quarrels and grumpy days. Our first parents now see the basest, ugliest desires of the human heart as they truly are. The truth of depravity is now laid bare in all its gore and hopelessness. There can be no more intellectual arguments about knowing right from wrong. Wrong has shown its true face. And it is the face of death.

In The Trenches

1. When we think of sin, we often think of telling lies, or not obeying, or being mean. These are all actions of a sinful heart. We forget that sinful thoughts can lead to very terrible actions. Jesus reminds us of this in his Sermon on the Mount. Read Matthew 5:21–22. What does Jesus say about the possible "fruit" of anger?

2. Why is sin so terrible?

Day 3

No Eden Here

I built a monastery,
A place to get away,
A refuge from the busy–ness,
The horrible,
And edginess of day.

But every trouble follows me,

Like clinging shadows,
wrestling my serenity from peace.
My energies I find expended,
Trying to keep my pains at bay.
They never cease.
No Eden here.

It looks like calm.
I have created sanctuary.
It looks like Eden from the outside looking in.
But from the inside looking out
the edginess and fear remain.

The earth is His,
And so it is.
An elegance of grace,
A glorious space.
But life itself is its façade.
Beneath the trees,
The layered plants,
The trampled dirt,
Is teeming,
Hot intensity,
Is swarming,
Growing,
Breathing Life,
Only deterred or redirected
by the constant hand of man,
Not sculpted carefully,
Life's very being marked by God's own infinite abundance.

And we, the stewards,
Making gardens,
Only push and nudge the edges
of His sovereignty around
from dirt to ground
because of weeds.
The cluttered,

Sharp reminder of our evil deeds.

We tampered with the Grand Command.
We chose ourselves to rule the earth.

The Living flows.
We cannot tame its eagerness.
For we are wounded,
Flawed and marred by our own pride.
We harbor death.
We gave it birth,
We nurtured it,
And so it grows
in our own gardens.
Swelling with an appetite as strong as grass between the rocks,
As strong as shoots that push up after forests burn,
As strong as hurricanes and earthquakes,
Toppling,
Destroying what people make or what we sow,
As hot as sun to starve a soul,
And make an arid emptiness reveal our weariness below,
Our edginess,
Our fear,
That human havens can't remove,
That monasteries can't untangle underneath.
No Eden here.

In The Trenches

1. In the Middle Ages, people who wanted to serve and obey God and get away from an evil world, would go live in a monastery. A monastery is a building made up of a community of people who want to worship and obey God. What does the poem tell us about the people who live there? About the world inside the monastery?

2. What if a group of Christians decided to set up their own town far away from the city and all its crime. They would not allow TV or radio. They would only read the Bible and good books. Would the town be like Eden before the fall? Why or why not?

Day 4

The Bard Sings

You cannot fix the heart of man,
The royal tyrant
running roughshod over all he sees.
You cannot stop his grasping hand,
Or crush the giant ego
wrapped around his bitter soul.

For he was made to follow greatness,
Grand hyperbole at his command.
He was created,
Born to rule,
Adventures daring to be told.

He is a tragedy in motion,
An Achilles waiting to be pierced,
An Oedipus already blinded
by the suicide he boldly chose.

And so the woes are all they're singing.
Judgments fall like slicing rain.
All the elements decry his coming,
All the people mourn his name.
No songs,
No dialogues,
No confrontations
can expunge the stench of death that lingers,
Sweats from every pore.
Ten thousand years of pride and mayhem
advertise degraded splendor.
Boasting lights the sky
like crackling neon's constant blinking.
On,
Then off,
Then on,

But only of what went on before.

No tender melodies expressed,
No heroes here,
No glorious lore.
His thoughts I know for I am he.
Who can deliver me from who I am,
This mind, this heart, this soul of death?

I have no breath,
No visions left for sympathies.

But much for sorrow
heaped on sorrow,
Shadows casting shadows,
Vapors crying out for heroes.

In The Trenches

This poem is about the loss of heroes. The speaker in the poem imagines he is Adam, longing to be a hero. But he needs a greater, better hero to come and rescue him from his rebellious heart. There are stories, real and imagined, of heroes all through history. Some real heroes have done great deeds. But they have also done very bad things, or had terrible thoughts.

Here is our hero:

"He was wounded for our transgressions; he was crushed for our iniquities; upon him was the chastisement that brought us peace, and with his stripes we are healed" (Isa 53:5).

Pray the prayer of David from Psalm 51:

"Have mercy on me, O God, according to your steadfast love; according to your abundant mercy blot out my transgressions. Wash me thoroughly from my iniquity, and cleanse me from my sin! For I know my transgressions, and my sin is ever before me. Against you, you only, have I sinned and done what is evil in your sight" (Ps 51:1–4).

Day 5

Unveiled

The dragon,
Riding high,
Comes spewing flame,
Comes seething,
Grinding teeth.

Who cares what name he cries?
For he is Self,
The Royal Me.
His sweeping wings,
His brilliant flash,
He looks like light
bedazzling eyes
(He hides the cutting scales beneath).

He whimpers,
Sobs,
That Right is his desire,
What I Want,
My needs,
My pleasures
should come first
before God's guilty truth.

But he is vicious tooth,
And claw,
And steely,
Piercing jaw,
A mesmerizing killer
born from hubris and rebellion,
Rising deep,
From Hell's own screaming core.

And you who serve

the broken,
bleeding,
risen Christ,
You are his war.

Heart Check

1. Why does the speaker finally notice the dragon? Why do you think he did not notice him before?

2. What separates our lives from living like dragons?

This has been a difficult book to write. In the process of editing questions and quotes, some of the sections became disjointed. Suddenly the academic writing about dragons became my personal battle with dragons. Frustration brought out my worst nature, making me stressed and angry. I wanted to put the project down. But I realized that spiritual warfare is at work, even when writing about spiritual warfare. Perhaps *because* I am writing about spiritual warfare. We are all fighting dragons, and they insert themselves into every aspect of our lives. I have asked God for forgiveness. Where do I go from there? The Holy Spirit sent me to Psalm 51:12. I am not to linger on my sin, but instead, joy in his salvation! I pray the same for you.

3. Read Psalm 51:4-12. What does it mean to confess our sins, according to these verses?

4. What has God promised us when we confess before him?

Battlegrounds

"There is a noise of war in the camp" (Exod 32:17b).

Week 6—God Has Not Forgotten

Day 1

Studying the Battle Plan

"And Adam knew his wife again, and she bore a son and called his name Seth, for she said, 'God has appointed for me another offspring instead of Abel, for Cain killed him.' To Seth also a son was born, and he called his name Enosh. At that time people began to call upon the name of the LORD" (Gen 4:25–26).

In The Trenches

1. Today's passage is about new beginnings. After he commits murder, God sends Cain away. He will not only be away from his family, but away from God. Cain doesn't want to be near God. He wants to be his own god. Why is this a terrible loss for Cain and his descendants?

2. Eve gives birth to Seth. Seth is the beginning of people who will worship and love God.

   Noah will come from the line of Seth. Read Genesis 6:9. Noah is still a sinner, like everyone else, but what does the Bible say about Noah's heart?

Day 2

Scouting the Territory

Around the age of twelve, my mother began the long and laborious task of teaching me to sew. It started with a treadle sewing machine; an adventure in concentrated coordination, where feet need one constant rhythm, and hands and eyes need another. Think of patting your head and rubbing your stomach while guiding a very sharp needle evenly between layers of fabric. And there is no reverse. Reverse means threads instantly broken, requiring a complex rethreading of the machine.

From there I graduated to an electric machine (so much easier!) and the process of creating tidy seams, sleeves, zippers, and the hours of ripping out mistakes until I got it right. I understand the garden of despair, spending many days in frustration over difficult dress pattern details, and the seemingly endless seam ripping. More than one dress took me months because I kept putting the project away, discouraged by the constant "re-do" lessons. Such were my adventures into the thorns and thistles of sewing.

By fourteen, I was on to the fine work—buttonholes, darning, and cross-stitching. My mother had me complete a traditional cross-stitch piece that still hangs in my home. It says, "Mine is a garden of hope, that good fruits I may bring to God's great harvesting." I look at my handiwork from long ago and realize how appropriate it is to this passage. No longer in Eden, Adam and Eve are beginning to understand life in the garden of despair. What was once joy has become difficult and full of frustration. There are weeds to pull, and thorns and thistles are permeating every part of their life. One son has already killed the other. Where is the hope in that?

In the middle of Adam and Eve's constant garden of despair, God has not forgotten them, or his promises. He gives them a garden of hope. He gives them Seth. Seth has a son named Enosh, which according to Bruce Waltke means "weakness."[1] We know this is a good sign, because verse 26 tells us, "At that time people began to call upon the name of the LORD." This is weakness in its best sense; a trust and dependence on God's power over human autonomy. It is a directed move away from "my will" to "thine." It includes some illustrious descendants: Enoch, who lived a life with such devotion to God that he did not die, but went directly into God's presence, and Noah, who is recorded as "a righteous man, blameless in his generation

1. Waltke, *Genesis*, 101.

. . . who walked with God" (Gen 6:9). These men were not perfect, but they, like their much later descendent David, could be considered men after God's own heart.

God has not forgotten. God will preserve his people. God will fulfill his promises. Seth, Enosh, Enoch, and Noah are good fruits, leading inexorably by God's sovereign will and power to a greater harvest: the Son promised will someday come, he will slay the dragon, and he will rescue his people from their sin.

I smile now, remembering dresses only worn once or twice because the garden of despair, the frustration in their making, took so many months that I had grown out of them before I could truly enjoy them. Some day we will look back on those thorns and thistles in our lives as only fading memories. For the garden of hope—the coming, the death, the resurrection, and the ascension of Christ—has begun a greater harvesting already; a certain present peace and joy, even in the middle of weeds, and a future of glorious and final redemption.

In The Trenches

1. What does today's story tell us about God?

2. Why is dependence on God the best thing?

Day 3

> "So I find it to be a law that when I want to do right, evil lies close at hand. For I delight in the law of God, in my inner being, but I see in my members another law waging war against the law of my mind and making me captive to the law of sin that dwells in my members. Wretched man that I am! Who will deliver me from this body of death? Thanks be to God through Jesus Christ our Lord! So then, I myself serve the law of God with my mind, but with my flesh I serve the law of sin" (Rom 7:21–25).

In The Trenches

1. The Apostle Paul tells us that the law is good. It tells us how to live and what God loves. But Paul also recognizes that even though he belongs

to Christ, and has been made right before God because of Christ's righteousness, he still sins because he has not yet been made perfect. That will come when this old world ends, and there is a new heaven and a new earth. For now, Paul knows that he still sins. The difference now is that he knows he is sinning and wants to stop. The person who does not belong to Christ doesn't realize he is a sinner, or doesn't care. Who is Paul's hope in his struggle?

2. Have you experienced the same feelings as Paul? Do you sin and wish you could keep from sinning? Read Romans 8:1–11. What is Christ's role in freeing us from sin? What is the role of the Holy Spirit? Does this encourage your daily walk with God?

Day 4

Lamentations of the gods

It should have stayed unborn,
This grievous weakness man created out of tasted sin,
One bite,
One mad, rebellious bite,
If only just to be like God,
To truly know the good from evil.

Without thought,
Without a fight.
No swords to guard the sacred grove,
No will to follow honor.
Only urges,
Carelessness of heart,
Desires
Rising high above all else,
And liars telling stories for themselves—
"It was her fault,
It was the snake,
It was the God, the One who Knows."

Now knowing, too,

These imaged creatures face portentous truth.
For knowledge like this knowledge
Does not gather gods,
But sucks the marrow out of bones.
It crushes,
Maims,
A multiplicity of shames,
An alienation spread so broad,
So instantly defacing self,
That soul and body shrink toward old,
And only re-creation could destroy its swelling cold.

Wretched man that I am!
Who will deliver me
from this body of death?

I sin!
I sin!
Oh, He Who Knows,
Know me.
Let re-creation's steady work begin.

In The Trenches

1. What does the poem say that sin does to us?
2. The poem quotes from Romans 7:24, the passage we read yesterday. How does the speaker encourage herself, knowing she is a sinner, but a sinner saved by the grace of Jesus Christ?

Day 5

Heart Check

1. Read 2 Peter 1:3-5.

2. You are being transformed into the image of God. What have you been given? How has it been given to you? How should this strengthen you when you feel overwhelmed by your sinful nature?

Week 7—Appetites

Day 1

Studying the Battle Plan

"When Isaac was old and his eyes were dim so that he could not see, he called Esau his older son and said to him, 'My son'; and he answered, 'Here I am.' He said, 'Behold, I am old; I do not know the day of my death. Now then, take your weapons, your quiver and your bow, and go out to the field and hunt game for me, and prepare for me delicious food, such as I love, and bring it to me so that I may eat, that my soul may bless you before I die.'

Now Rebekah was listening when Isaac spoke to his son Esau. So when Esau went to the field to hunt for game and bring it, Rebekah said to her son Jacob, 'I heard your father speak to your brother Esau, "Bring me game and prepare for me delicious food, that I may eat it and bless you before the LORD before I die." Now therefore, my son, obey my voice as I command you. Go to the flock and bring me two good young goats, so that I may prepare from them delicious food for your father, such as he loves. And you shall bring it to your father to eat, so that he may bless you before he dies.' But Jacob said to Rebekah his mother, 'Behold, my brother Esau is a hairy man, and I am a smooth man. Perhaps my father will feel me, and I shall seem to be mocking him and bring a curse upon myself and not a blessing.' His mother said to him, 'Let your curse be on me, my son; only obey my voice, and go, bring them to me'" (Gen 27:1–13).

In The Trenches

1. Esau and Jacob are twins. Esau was born first. The firstborn son is the son who inherits the double portion and is responsible for the family. He has the position of authority. God had promised Grandfather Abraham that he would send a firstborn to redeem his people. The firstborn is all about God's faithful promises. But from the very beginning, Esau and Jacob have been fighting over who is entitled to both the position, and all its benefits. Even in the womb, the boys were wrestling each other. (Gen 25:22) And Esau was willing to trade away his privilege and his sacred heritage to Jacob for a bowl of lentil stew. (Gen 25:29–34) Look at their parents. Are Isaac and Rebekah working as a team?

2. Jacob reminds me of Eve talking to the serpent. He is already considering his mother's idea and identifying problems that need to be addressed. What should Jacob have said to his mother?

Day 2

Scouting the Territory

Isaac reminds me of my second grade teacher—colorless, almost invisible, a mere bridge between two more memorable individuals. I learned good handwriting skills from my second grade teacher, but not much else. I can't even remember her name. It has been more than fifty years since elementary school, and I can still vividly remember my first and third grade teachers. Second grade is a gray memory. Isaac reads like a gray memory, in between two vibrant, yet flawed powerhouses—Abraham and Jacob.

But Isaac did teach one thing well to both his sons: to live by their appetites. Esau is ruled, like his father, by his desire for comfort food. Jacob, who is good at "reading" his twin, wants position, and knows how to get it. Read Genesis 25:29–34. Trading the birthright for hot stew was an easy bargain. Now mom is pushing for the firstborn's blessing. Hadn't the LORD already promised it would go to Jacob? Surely Isaac was aware of the prophecy given to Rebekah back in Genesis 25:22–23 while she was waiting for her warring sons in the womb to be born—"So she went to inquire of the LORD. And the LORD said to her, 'Two nations are in your womb, and two peoples from within you shall be divided; the one shall be stronger than the other, the older shall serve the younger.'"

The older shall serve the younger. The text goes straight to the heart of the problem—"Isaac loved Esau because he ate of his game, but Rebekah loved Jacob" (Gen 25:28). Esau was a man's man, the skillful hunter. He and his father loved to eat good meat. Jacob was "a quiet man, dwelling in tents" (Gen 25:27). He was hanging around the women all day. Each parent had a son that appealed to that parent's appetites and interests.

Yes, God had promised that the older would serve the younger. But Isaac, Rebekah, and Jacob, the players in this drama, are all about brokering deals to their advantage. They do not trust God to work through their flaws and situation, or give them the grace and direction to accept his solution.

Isaac is invisible because his vision is small. And his physical blindness expresses a metaphor of his spiritual condition. He (and his wife in her own way), is resting in what he can get, not what God has promised. They are back at Genesis 3, standing before the serpent in the garden, weighing their options against God's will and choosing to scratch their own way out—what looks good, what feels good, what feeds me first. Appetites—perhaps that is why there is so little said about Isaac.

In The Trenches

1. What is wrong with living by our appetites?

2. The LORD had already promised Rebekah that Jacob, her favorite, would be the stronger son. What should she have done differently? Who was she trusting in?

Day 3

Studying the Battle Plan

"Therefore I tell you, do not be anxious about your life, what you will eat or what you will drink, nor about your body, what you will put on. Is not life more than food, and the body more than clothing? Look at the birds of the air: they neither sow nor reap nor gather into barns, and yet your heavenly Father feeds them. Are you not of more value than they? And which of you by being anxious can add a single hour to his span of life? And why are you anxious about clothing? Consider the lilies of the field, how they grow: they neither toil nor spin, yet I tell you, even Solomon in all his glory was not arrayed like one of these. But if God so clothes the grass of the field, which today is alive and tomorrow is thrown into the oven, will he not much more clothe you, O you of little faith? Therefore do not be anxious, saying, 'What shall we eat?' or 'What shall we drink?' or 'What shall we wear?' For the Gentiles seek after all these things, and your heavenly Father knows that you need them all. But seek first the kingdom of God and his righteousness, and all these things will be added to you."(Matt 6:25–33)

In The Trenches

1. The opposite of living by appetites (me first) is to live by faith (God first). What examples does Jesus give us to encourage us to trust in God to meet our needs?

2. What does it mean to seek first the kingdom of God? How should that change the way we live?

Day 4

Of the Stomach

I grieve her sin and mine,
My storm of anger
over what
she so easily gives up.
For Self,
For stubbornness,
She squanders life.
So short,
So fleeting,
Passing both us by,
Exchanging appetites for joy,
Not willing to extend
beyond immediacy,

A Settled Life.

Yet God can even lift this up,
This settledness,
My stubborn hurt,
And shake awake
a hungry heart for better things.

And lovingly,
With great compassion,
Elevate such meager souls
to sing doxologies of grace before His plate,
His dinner table's bread and wine.

He takes our hurt,
(My pain and hers).
For only His own sacrifice
releases empty tongues at last
(which could not taste),
To savor His eternity.

In The Trenches

1. What does the speaker say is the consequence of living by our appetites?

2. The poem gives us an alternative with an "eating" metaphor. It compares the eating of communion to express the right kind of "eating." What does communion symbolize? What should our taking of the bread and wine say about our relationship with Christ? What should we be "eating"? Hint: Read Deuteronomy 8: 1–3.

Day 5

Heart Check

"So, whether you eat or drink, or whatever you do, do all to the glory of God" (1 Cor 10:31).

1. Thinking about the poem, "*Of the Stomach*," what does it mean to eat or drink to the glory of God?

2. Paul takes the idea even farther in the whole section of 1 Corinthians 10:23–33. He tells us that just because some kinds of appetites are considered acceptable, we need to think about appetites that could hurt and weaken a friend's faith. Meats sold in the open market in Paul's day had sometimes been first offered to pagan gods, before being bought and served for dinner. What if your friend came over to eat hamburgers and discovered that he was eating meat offered to false gods, and he thought it was wrong? Is it better to first think about our own comfort, or about the faith of a friend? Why?

Week 8—Little Gods

Day 1

Studying the Battle Plan

"Then Rebekah took the best garments of Esau her older son, which were with her in the house, and put them on Jacob her younger son. And the skins of the young goats she put on his hands and on the smooth part of his neck. And she put the delicious food and the bread, which she had prepared, into the hand of her son Jacob.

So he went in to his father and said, 'My father.' And he said, 'Here I am. Who are you, my son?' Jacob said to his father, 'I am Esau your firstborn. I have done as you told me; now sit up and eat of my game, that your soul may bless me.' But Isaac said to his son, 'How is it that you have found it so quickly, my son?' He answered, 'Because the LORD your God granted me success.' Then Isaac said to Jacob, 'Please come near, that I may feel you, my son, to know whether you are really my son Esau or not.' So Jacob went near to Isaac his father, who felt him and said, 'The voice is Jacob's voice, but the hands are the hands of Esau.' And he did not recognize him, because his hands were hairy like his brother Esau's hands. So he blessed him. He said, 'Are you really my son Esau?' He answered, 'I am.' Then he said, 'Bring it near to me, that I may eat of my son's game and bless you.' So he brought it near to him, and he ate; and he brought him wine, and he drank" (Gen 27:15–25).

In The Trenches

1. Rebekah and Jacob go to a great deal of trouble to deceive. What are all the things they did to make Isaac believe he was speaking to Esau and not to Jacob?

2. Isaac is blind, so he cannot really see which son is with him. How does Isaac identify Jacob as Esau? Even though God promised that in the end Esau's descendants would serve Jacob's descendants, were Jacob and Rebekah right or wrong in what they did?

Day 2

Scouting the Territory

Welcome to the world of other gods, little gods, the gods created by us. Isaac worships the comforts that food and a successful son provide. Isaac worships control. And Esau in turn worships the love of his father, and his own hunting prowess. Rebekah worships the power and control that comes from being the favored mom behind the important son. She remembers the prophecy, and revels in the job of "king maker." She will not wait on the God's provision, but manage fulfillment herself. Jacob worships the attention of his mother and the opportunity to get for himself the perks of inheritance—the birthright and the blessing. Worship of little gods make people battle each other instead of the true enemies around them.

How do I know they are at war with each other? Three things stand out in this passage, and they revolve around the simple statement Jacob made in Genesis 27:20b, "Because the LORD your God granted me success." Neither Jacob nor Isaac recognize the dissonance in the air. First, Jacob is lying about where the food came from, and putting a religious whitewash on it to make it sound not only plausible, but acceptable. Second, it is only a whitewash because this son wants the blessing, but not the God of his fathers. "The LORD *your* God," he says. He'll take anything and everything he can get from his father, but he's not buying into his dad's religion. He'll dress the part, say the right words, and do what is required; everything except claim the LORD as his own. Bruce Waltke comments, "Jacob has no qualms about the morality of the plan, only about its feasibility."[1] As far as his mother's plan is concerned, he is agreeably cold and calculating. Third, Isaac is so eager for the food and a chance to take personal control of the direction of God's prophecy, he hasn't been paying much attention to what Jacob just said. "Your God" should have been a red flag. But then maybe Isaac isn't as connected to the Lord either. Or he doesn't have any expectations that his son Esau (remember, he thinks he is talking to Esau) will follow in the ways of Grandfather Abraham. Yet he still wants to confer that holy blessing on this son. Somehow, he does believe in the blessing. But he wants to give it away on his own terms.

What kind of marriage, what kind of upbringing, influenced this household? And is anybody worshipping the God of Abraham? Why is the woman designing and executing a battle strategy against the will of her husband? Why is the hero of her battle a thief? Why is the spiritual ruler of this story so blind in so many ways? And why are we reading about this dysfunctional family? Why? Because they are not only a real, historical family, living out their own reckless stratagems, they are also us—liars, cheats, and manipulators. All calculating what is needed to control our own little kingdoms, irrespective of the costs. And there are costs. Esau doesn't change, but grows further from the truth. Rebekah disappears from the story line. "Ominously," writes Waltke, "she disappears . . . after this scene. The narrator memorializes Deborah, her nurse, not Rebekah and makes no notice of her death."[2] And mom's favorite is nowhere on the scene when she dies. Jacob, because of his actions, will be forced to flee.

What is holding God's promises together in such a wasted mess? God is. And this is the main reason why we should read their story—because it is not only their story, but God's story to each of us. God's promises cannot be thwarted no matter what man does. And he revels in rescuing and redeeming weak and wayward people for his royal house. Why else would Jacob be able to truly fulfill the promise? He does not have the character of a leader, or the heart of a king. And he certainly is not Esau's better by any standard. But God is bigger and grander than this conniving man. And the blessing will hold fast. It will never be broken. A king will come, one who will mortally wound the head of the serpent. And Jacob, amazingly, is being given a share in this victory. For a great King will come from this weak and wretched line, a line God is choosing, changing, and growing into a people

1. Waltke, *Genesis*, 378.
2. Waltke, Ibid., 378.

of faith, as descendants one by one put their faith in the bloody sacrifice of this King still to come. Through the power of the Holy Spirit they throw away their little gods in worship of the living God. And one day, not by might, nor by power, nor by human stratagems, but by the Spirit of this living God, a glorious, dragon-slaying savior will be born.

In The Trenches

1. What happens when we worship little gods instead of God?

2. Read Isaiah 55:8–11 and Philippians 1:6. How can we have confidence that God's will cannot be thwarted by us or by anyone else?

Day 3

Postings from the Front

"If we insist on keeping Hell (or even Earth) we shall not see Heaven: If we accept Heaven we shall not be able to retain even the smallest and most intimate souvenirs of Hell . . . I think earth, if chosen instead of Heaven, will turn out to have been, all along, only a region in Hell: and earth, if put second to Heaven, to have been from the beginning, a part of Heaven itself."— C.S. Lewis.[3]

In The Trenches

1. We as humans have the ability to make idols out of anything and everything. Even religion, without the relationship with Christ, can become an idol. How could even church become an idol?

2. Read Exodus 20:1–11. These verses are the first half of the Ten Commandments. What does God say about worshipping him?

---

3. Lewis, Preface, *Great Divorce*, 6–7.

Day 4

Ichabod

We are the forgetting,
The nameless.
Wisdom and glory long ago departed.

We had a name.
I think we had a name,
Deserved a name.

Now we all are brooding thoughts.
Fleeting,
Vacuous thoughts
and feelings,
Rising,
Dancing like October's disconnected,
Dying leaves,
Their brittle boredom caught up,
Blown by every wind of doctrine,
Scattered,
Lost.

I thought I had a name.
I guess it can't be found.

Fallen,
Fallen is Babylon!
And all the carved images of her gods
He has scattered to the ground.

In The Trenches

The name Ichabod means, "Where is the glory?" Ichabod was a baby boy born in the early years of Israel, when Samuel was God's prophet (1 Sam 4). During that time, the ark of the covenant, an ornately figured gold box, was intended to stay in the temple in Shiloh as a visible sign of God's presence with his people. Instead, the Israelites had taken it into battle. The people of Israel mistakenly believed they could make God bring them victory if they brought the box with them. Israel's enemies defeated Israel, and captured the box and took it away. The baby's father died in battle. His grandfather died when he heard the ark had been taken. Ichabod was born into a world where God's presence had left Israel. To "have a name" is to say you belong to someone.

1. How does the poem express the loss of God's presence?

2. What does C.S. Lewis mean when he says that, "I think earth, if chosen instead of Heaven, will turn out to have been, all along, only a region in Hell: and earth, if put second to Heaven, to have been from the beginning, a part of heaven itself."[4] How does that fit with the poem?

Day 5

Heart Check

1. Read Matthew 6:19–21.

2. Do you get angry when you cannot have something you think you deserve? Be careful, you just described a treasure. Will this treasure you think you need so much last forever? If not, it may be dragon hoard.

4. Lewis, Preface, *Great Divorce*, 7.

Week 9—Hearts Revealed

Day 1

Studying the Battle Plan

"As soon as Isaac had finished blessing Jacob, when Jacob had scarcely gone out from the presence of Isaac his father, Esau his brother came in from his hunting. He also prepared delicious food and brought it to his father. And he said to his father, 'Let my father arise and eat of his son's game, that you may bless me.' His father Isaac said to him, 'Who are you?' He answered, 'I am your son, your firstborn, Esau.' Then Isaac trembled very violently and said, 'Who was it then that hunted game and brought it to me, and I ate it all before you came, and I have blessed him? Yes, and he shall be blessed.' As soon as Esau heard the words of his father he cried out with an exceedingly great and bitter cry and said to his father, 'Bless me, even me also, O my father!' But he said, 'Your brother came deceitfully, and he has taken away your blessing.' Esau said, 'Is he not rightly named Jacob? For he has cheated me these two times. He took away my birthright, and behold, now he has taken away my blessing.' Then he said, 'Have you not reserved a blessing for me?' Isaac answered and said to Esau, 'Behold, I have made him lord over you, and all his brothers I have given to him for servants, and with grain and wine I have sustained him. What then can I do for you, my son?' Esau said to his father, 'Have you but one blessing, my father? Bless me, even me also, O my father.' And Esau lifted up his voice and wept." (Gen 27:30–38)

In The Trenches

1. Read the first paragraph of the passage. Now read Genesis 12:1–3. How is God's blessing on Abram (Abraham) like Isaac's blessing on Jacob (disguised as Esau)?

2. Isaac thinks he has beaten God at his own game. He believes he has given the blessing God meant for Jacob to Esau instead. How does Isaac's blessing fulfill God's revelation to Rebekah in Genesis 25:23? Can we ever thwart God's holy will?

3. Now read the rest of the passage. What a dramatic reveal! "Esau" is actually Jacob, and the blessing for the firstborn has been given away. Isaac cannot take the blessing back. It is given. What blessing can he offer to Esau? (Read Genesis 27:39–40).

Day 2

Scouting the Territory

Isaac trembled violently. He had forgotten for a moment that he was always in the presence of a holy God. The man who schemed to consign the blessing his way, recognized immediately not only the futility of imposing his will over God's, but that he was now in a very dangerous position before the sovereign ruler of heaven and earth. "Isaac was sufficiently a man of faith to recognize his mistake once it was exposed," agrees Ian Duguid (Professor of Old Testament at Westminster Theological Seminary, Philadelphia). "Isaac trembled . . . because his wrong intentions had been exposed and defeated by God's sovereignty. So when Esau sought a further blessing, Isaac had none to give. He would not try to thwart God a second time."[1] Isaac may have been foolish and wayward, but he was also the man who had prayed for his wife, earlier in their marriage, when she had been barren, and "the LORD had granted his prayer" (Gen 25:21). He is the man who met God at Beersheba, and built an altar there, where "he called upon the name of the LORD" (Gen 26:25), responding to God's reiteration of the covenant promise he had given to Abraham, now offered to the son. "The bearers of Christ's kingdom," writes Bruce Waltke, "are sometimes strong and some-

---

1. Duguid, *Living in the Grip*, 39–40.

times weak."[2] Isaac's allegiance to God was weak, and it twisted and turned according to his passions. But the blessing Isaac bestowed on Jacob (even unwittingly), is full of God's promises to his people, and Isaac's visceral response to being found out at least hints at where he knew his heart should be.

Where the father trembled, the son blamed and raged. In the midst of his loss, Esau's heart and his loyalties are exposed. In Esau's faulty memory, Jacob stole the birthright as well as the blessing that Esau craved. Esau has already forgotten how easily he had given up the birthright for stew. "I am about to die," he cried dramatically; "of what use is a birthright to me?" (Gen 25:32) Who cares about tomorrow when I live for my stomach today? Genesis tells us Esau "despised his birthright" (Gen 25:34b). Hebrews 12 calls Esau "unholy," because he so easily disdained his birthright. His disdain was a rejection of his inheritance. And when he wanted the blessing, and couldn't have it either, he became angry and vengeful. His desire turned toward premeditated murder, not repentance. Esau's allegiance is to Esau alone. He is bitter and planning to kill.

The father falters, the sons fail. None of the men in this sordid tale seem to be men after God's own heart. None deserve God's covenant blessing. But that is just the point. They do not deserve it. We do not deserve it. The amazing part of this story is that the blessing has always been bigger than the dew of heaven and the fat of the earth. It is a blessing of eternal mercy promised and granted to the forever undeserving. The human heart cannot survive the battle. Only the heart of God, broken and crushed for us, absorbing the horrors of our hearts at the cross, saves any of us. God is the one holding Isaac's heart, not letting it stray, preventing this father from fulfilling his own desires. God will not let go of Jacob, but patiently and firmly, over a lifetime of battle, will turn the deceiver's heart toward the Righteous King. God is always aware of the battle. We may not even notice how our weaknesses twist and knot our frustrations into allegiances against God himself. He knows. He is always at work; untying, undoing, restoring. He holds on to our proud, fearful, angry, and despairing hearts, and he never lets go.

2. Waltke, *Genesis*, 372.

In The Trenches

1. According to Dr. Duguid, why did Isaac tremble when faced with Jacob's deceit? What did he recognize about himself and God?
2. How did Esau's response differ? What does it say about Esau's heart?

Day 3

Do Not Feed Your Dragons

They whisper at your elbow,
Sniffing air for envies,
Brutish odors,
Lingering distrust and malice,
Waiting until ripening occurs.

And these—
Malevolence incarnate,
Nudge and press against like starving dogs,
Miseries of hunger,
Lost,
They prowl and pace
with wanting undeterred.

They seek your dark.
Beware!
Desire begs to swallow you.

You must resist.
Don't give an inch.

Did God really say you shall not eat?
The Sting!
The hit!
The dragon has already bit!

In The Trenches

1. In this poem, dragons are a metaphor, a picture of all things evil or sinful in this world that would pull us away from God. What sin pulled Isaac away from obeying God?

2. Whether the dragons are outside of us, or prowling in our own hearts and thoughts, the intention is to destroy us. Dragon thoughts pulled Esau away from God. But Jacob's dragonish behavior also pulled Isaac back to God when Isaac's sinful heart was revealed. Why is this? Read Romans 9:6–16. All men are sinners. All deserve destruction. Yet God, in his mercy, rescues many. God chose to rescue Isaac, even though Isaac did not deserve to be rescued. It is an amazing thought.

Day 4

Studying the Battle Plan

"But this is the covenant that I will make with the house of Israel after those days, declares the LORD: I will put my law within them, and I will write it on their hearts. And I will be their God, and they shall be my people. And no longer shall each one teach his neighbor and each his brother, saying, 'Know the LORD,' for they shall all know me, from the least of them to the greatest, declares the LORD. For I will forgive their iniquity, and I will remember their sin no more" (Jer 31:33–34).

In The Trenches

1. Read Jeremiah 31:33–34; also read John 16:7–15. In the Old Testament, the people of God are looking forward to the coming firstborn, the Dragon Slayer who will free them from sin and teach their hearts to obey and love God. How will all of Jeremiah 31:33–34 be fulfilled?

2. What then is our hope as we fight against our own dragonish thoughts and actions?

Day 5

Heart Check

What if all my treasures are dragon treasures? Will God still win? Yes! Remember that you are being changed, in spite of yourself!

> "As you come to him, a living stone rejected by men but in the sight of God chosen and precious, you yourselves like living stones are being built up as a spiritual house, to be a holy priesthood, to offer spiritual sacrifices acceptable to God through Jesus Christ" (1 Pet 2:4–5).

Week 10—Super Powers

Day 1

Studying the Battle Plan

"And the messengers returned to Jacob, saying, 'We came to your brother Esau, and he is coming to meet you, and there are four hundred men with him.' Then Jacob was greatly afraid and distressed. He divided the people who were with him, and the flocks and herds and camels, into two camps, thinking, 'If Esau comes to the one camp and attacks it, then the camp that is left will escape.'

And Jacob said, 'O God of my father Abraham and God of my father Isaac, O LORD who said to me, "Return to your country and to your kindred, that I may do you good," I am not worthy of the least of all the deeds of steadfast love and all the faithfulness that you have shown to your servant, for with only my staff I crossed this Jordan, and now I have become two camps. Please deliver me from the hand of my brother, from the hand of Esau, for I fear him, that he may come and attack me, the mothers with the children. But you said, "I will surely do you good, and make your offspring as the sand of the sea, which cannot be numbered for multitude."'

So he stayed there that night, and from what he had with him he took a present for his brother Esau, two hundred female goats and twenty male goats, two hundred ewes and twenty rams, thirty milking camels and their calves, forty cows and ten bulls, twenty female donkeys and ten male donkeys. These he handed over to his servants, every drove by itself, and said to his servants, 'Pass on ahead of me and put a space between drove and drove.' He instructed the first, 'When Esau my brother meets you and asks you,

61

"To whom do you belong? Where are you going? And whose are these ahead of you?" then you shall say, "They belong to your servant Jacob. They are a present sent to my lord Esau. And moreover, he is behind us.'" He likewise instructed the second and the third and all who followed the droves, 'You shall say the same thing to Esau when you find him, and you shall say, "Moreover, your servant Jacob is behind us."' For he thought, 'I may appease him with the present that goes ahead of me, and afterward I shall see his face. Perhaps he will accept me.' So the present passed on ahead of him, and he himself stayed that night in the camp" (Gen 32:6–21).

In The Trenches

1. Many years have passed since Jacob deceived Esau. Jacob had been quickly sent away to relatives to escape Esau's wrath. Now, years later, both brothers have raised families, and have built up enormous wealth and power. Part of wealth and power in the days of the patriarchs was to have a great army of men at your disposal to protect people and property. Jacob and Esau each had huge camps of supplies, many family members, a host of servants, an army of fighting men, and vast amounts of livestock. They traveled around the land, to make sure their flocks of goats, sheep, donkeys, and oxen had plenty of grasses to eat. Jacob hears that Esau is coming his way and he remembers the angry brother he left behind. He remembers how he deceived his brother. He also hears that Esau is heading toward him with an army of 400 men. Jacob is afraid. He has spent his whole life wheeling and dealing his way through every problem. Read the passage. In what way has Jacob not changed from the way he was as a young man?

2. Look at the passage again. How is Jacob's heart changing?

Day 2

Scouting the Territory

I am afraid of fire. One of my most intense experiences with this element was as a five–year–old child. My kindergarten teacher was demonstrating fire's need for oxygen by lighting a candle, and then covering the open flame with a glass bell jar. She could never get past the lighting of the candle without me bursting into tears. In my fearful imagination, the whole class-room and all of its inhabitants were about to be consumed. She wisely commanded me to come up to the front of the class and place the bell jar over the flame. It was an overwhelmingly fearful moment. With sweaty, shaking hands, I faced my enemy and brought the bell jar down over the flame. If there was an intensity of fearful dread when I stood before my fiery nemesis, there was an equally intense emotion of triumph as the flame sputtered out. I had conquered fire! What glorious powers were at my command! It was a heady moment, and I could hardly wait to get home and demonstrate my prowess to my parents.

With my mother watching with understandable trepidation, I lit the candle, brought a large canning jar down on the flickering flame, accidently knocked the whole experiment of glory over in my excitement, and promptly set the kitchen counter on fire! My mother immediately smothered her smoldering countertop, and my super powers instantly burned away into ashes. Fire, it seems, was much bigger than I had previously thought or even imagined. I had a faulty picture of the size of the problem and my ability to overcome it. There is a healthy fear of fire's ability to destroy, and an equally healthy understanding of how one can properly handle it. I had neither.

Incorrect assessments of fearful situations are not limited to five-year-olds. Jacob was an older man with a large family and years of human experience. Yet here he was, facing meeting the one person he feared the most; the brother he had badly deceived twenty years earlier and who had threatened to murder him. Familial memories and relationship patterns from long ago probably came flooding back, and Jacob was once more the manipulator fleeing from a vengeful brother. And this time, his brother was marching toward him with an army of four hundred men. When there is nowhere to run, what do you do? Jacob saw the fires ahead and did what Jacob always did—he went for the bluff and the manipulation. He divided his large entourage into two camps. If one was lost, perhaps the other might escape unharmed. He sent extravagant gifts ahead to placate, with messengers to flatter his adversary. He depended on his own super powers to put out the flames.

He did pray, but even here he was depending on his well-honed powers of manipulation. "You promised me that you would take care of me," he reminded God. He made sure in his prayer to mention those mothers and children in the path of revenge. It is telling that God is still addressed as the God "of my father Abraham and God of my father Isaac" (Gen 32:9). It sounds religious, but Yahweh is not yet Jacob's God. Yahweh is old family stories of glory and promises, not a relationship of love and faithfulness.

Jacob doesn't need super powers. He needs to trust in the one with all the power. Like me, he needed a healthy understanding of his true abilities and a clear picture of the situation. Life is full of uncontrollable situations that threaten to ravage our lives. And all our super powers are merely ash. Only God can put out these kinds of fires, and it is eminently useful to stop in the midst of our trials and remember this. Bell jars and super powers don't even come close. All we get is burned countertops.

Stop. Trust him. Wait on his solution and rest in it.

In The Trenches

1. Why do you think the title of Week 10 is Super Powers?

2. What did I learn about fear as a five-year-old?

3. What does Jacob need to meet Esau?

Day 3

Read these verses and consider memorizing them to remind you of God's powerful care for you:

Deuteronomy 31:6; Joshua 1:9; Joshua 24:14; Psalm 27:1; Psalm 56:3; Psalm 118:6; Isaiah 44:8.

In The Trenches

1. Who is in control of your life?

2. What does it mean to trust God?

Day 4

Postings from the Front

"Suffering *feels* like our biggest problem and avoiding it like our greatest need—but we know there is something more. Sin is actually our biggest problem, and rescue from it is our greatest need."—Edward T. Welch.[1]

"A woman went through a deep depression. She hoped and prayed for deliverance, but she didn't receive it, at least not in the way she desired. Instead, depression raged for months that felt like lifetimes before it finally lifted. Now she is headed down that same downhill course again. Yet what should terrorize her is actually being welcomed. As she looks back on her previous depression, she can see deliverance in a way she didn't expect: God gave her the gift of faith to cling tenaciously to the One who holds her. Yes, it takes a certain amount of spiritual maturity to appreciate such things, but even those who know her recognize that she has been transformed into an increasingly glorious woman through her trials. She has seen a redemptive deliverance. The thing she feared did happen, but God did something in her in the midst of it that she recognized was for her good and his glory. It was worth it to her."—Edward T. Welch[2]

In The Trenches

1. Dr. Welch's quote tells us of a woman whose worst fear did actually come true. Why does he say it was worth it for her to go through this difficult experience?

2. How are we to view suffering? How are we to view sin?

3. Why do you suppose that God is allowing Jacob to go through his experience?

Day 5

Heart Check?

1. Read Isaiah 26:3–4.

2. How can we find peace?

3. What does it mean to trust? Why can we trust?

1. Welch, *Side By Side*, 43.
2. Welch, *Running Scared*, 90.

Week 11—Family Reunions

Day 1

Studying the Battle Plan

"The same night he arose and took his two wives, his two female servants, and his eleven children, and crossed the ford of the Jabbok. He took them and sent them across the stream, and everything else that he had. And Jacob was left alone. And a man wrestled with him until the breaking of the day. When the man saw that he did not prevail against Jacob, he touched his hip socket, and Jacob's hip was put out of joint as he wrestled with him. Then he said, 'Let me go, for the day has broken.' But Jacob said, 'I will not let you go unless you bless me.' And he said to him, 'What is your name?' And he said, 'Jacob.' Then he said, 'Your name shall no longer be called Jacob, but Israel, for you have striven with God and with men, and have prevailed.' Then Jacob asked him, 'Please tell me your name.' But he said, 'Why is it that you ask my name?' And there he blessed him. So Jacob called the name of the place Peniel, saying, 'For I have seen God face to face, and yet my life has been delivered.' The sun rose upon him as he passed Penuel, limping because of his hip." (Gen 32:22–31)

In The Trenches

1. Was it more important to meet Esau or to meet God? Why?
2. Why do you think God permanently crippled Jacob's hip?

Day 2

Studying the Battle Plan

"And Jacob lifted up his eyes and looked, and behold, Esau was coming, and four hundred men with him. So he divided the children among Leah and Rachel and the two female servants. And he put the servants with their children in front, then Leah with her children, and Rachel and Joseph last of all. He himself went on before them, bowing himself to the ground seven times, until he came near to his brother.

But Esau ran to meet him and embraced him and fell on his neck and kissed him, and they wept. And when Esau lifted up his eyes and saw the women and children, he said, 'Who are these with you?' Jacob said, 'The children whom God has graciously given your servant.' Then the servants drew near, they and their children, and bowed down. Leah likewise and her children drew near and bowed down. And last Joseph and Rachel drew near, and they bowed down. Esau said, 'What do you mean by all this company that I met?' Jacob answered, 'To find favor in the sight of my lord.' But Esau said, 'I have enough, my brother; keep what you have for yourself.' Jacob said, 'No, please, if I have found favor in your sight, then accept my present from my hand. For I have seen your face, which is like seeing the face of God, and you have accepted me. Please accept my blessing that is brought to you, because God has dealt graciously with me, and because I have enough.' Thus he urged him, and he took it." (Gen 33:1–11)

In The Trenches

1. Originally, Jacob planned to walk at the end of the group to meet Esau. Why do you think Jacob decided instead to walk at the front of the family group?

2. What an amazing reunion! Who reaches out to whom first?

3. Jacob tells his brother he has enough. After a lifetime of trying to beat the system to get more, he says he has enough. Why does he say this?

Day 3

Scouting the Territory

When my husband was a toddler and his mother asked if he needed any help, he would say, "I do it mine-self." Jacob was all about "mine-self." He had been living off stratagems for twenty years. From stealing his brother's blessing, to intrigues with in-laws in the matter of collecting wives and flocks of goats, Jacob was always a "get-by-or-run" kind of guy. Over the past twenty years, he had collected lots of stuff, gained two contentiously competitive wives, and a houseful of undisciplined sons. What was intended to be a route back home, the place he had fled so many years earlier, was turning rapidly into another "get-by-or-run" scheme. Esau was approaching with four hundred men, and Jacob's response was flattery, gifts, and schemes. He was a man looking for leverage.

But that's not how God works. God initiates. God intrudes. God changes the game. God suddenly came upon Jacob in the form of a man and wrestled him to the ground, wrestling all night. I am told that a man's legs provide support and power when he wrestles. They are his leverage. If you don't have legs when you wrestle, you will lose. God literally took Jacob's leverage, his sense of cocky "mine-self" away. He permanently dislocated Jacob's hip, so that Jacob couldn't fight. He could only cling. And that's just what Jacob needed. He clung to God and said he would not let go without a blessing. And God gave him a rich blessing. God changed Jacob. God claimed Jacob. He let Jacob live. "I have seen God face to face, and yet my life has been delivered" (Gen 32:30). He gave Jacob a new name—Israel, which means, "strives with God." After wrestling the God of the universe and surviving, what was the point of all the rest? For the rest of his life, Jacob's limp would remind him that he couldn't manage on his own, that he was intended to lean on God.

The Jacob that meets Esau is a different man. Before, he was planning on being the last in line, with family, possessions, presents, and flattery all up front. Now he gathered his family and walked in front of them, bowing seven times before his brother. It was the right way to meet after so many years, and Esau rushed to embrace his twin, and they both wept.

"Mine-self" has been the fallback position for humanity ever since that first fateful bite in the garden. But our weakness is one of God's favorite methods of rescue. When life throws its worst, sometimes God uses our trials to wrestle us to the ground. And sometimes a part of our life becomes dislocated permanently. We become weak. We can't fight. We can only cling to him. But clinging to the Lord is the safest place in the world. Clinging to the Lord is where we gain his wisdom and strength. We weren't created to manage on our own. He knows we are much too often a "mine–self" kind of people, so he puts us in positions that force us to cling to him. And then he blesses us. "My grace is sufficient for you," God says, "for my power is made perfect in weakness." "Therefore," exalts the apostle Paul in 2 Corinthians 12, "I will boast all the more gladly of my weaknesses, so that the power of Christ may rest upon me . . . For when I am weak, then I am strong." Jacob with a limp is a stronger, wiser man; a man properly prepared to face Esau. Jacob is a reconciled and reconciling man who is freed to forgive and be forgiven. Because he left his leverage on the field of battle with the God of the universe, there will be no more battles to be fought with Esau. They will meet again one more time to bury their father Isaac, and then go home.

In The Trenches

1. Read Exodus 33:18–23. Jacob changed the name the place of his meeting with God to *Peniel*, which means "the face of God." After reading about Moses' meeting with God, why is Jacob's meeting so significant?

2. What does this say about God's holiness? What does it say about his mercy?

Day 4

Studying the Battle Plan

"The fear of the LORD is the beginning of wisdom, and the knowledge of the Holy One is insight" (Prov 9:10).

In The Trenches

1. How did God change Jacob's perspective on life? How do we know Jacob is a changed man?

2. "Mine–self" is dragon language. It is the language of hoarding, of putting my needs first. How does God get mine–self out of our hearts?

Day 5

Heart Check

For the Lost

O LORD,
Creator,
LORD, the LORD,
Most merciful and gracious Being,
Slow to anger,
Ever seeing,
Always faithful,
Overflowing steadfast love,
Forgive.
Forgive.

Untie the knots
that bind these hearts
to Not My People.

Melt our vacuous cold,
Like ice,
Adorning,
Chilling soul.

Unmask oppression's glitter.
Burn its treachery.
Reveal your Name again,
And make us whole.

We plead for mercy,

LORD, we plead,

And lay our lives,

Your bride,

Before your throne.

"But now thus says the LORD, he who created you, O Jacob, he who formed you, O Israel: 'Fear not, for I have redeemed you; I have called you by name, you are mine.'" (Isa 43:1)

Put your name in the place of Jacob and Israel and repeat this verse. When it is not about "me," but is all about God, does this give you hope?

Week 12—Good Fear

Day 1

Studying the Battle Plan

"And Saul said to David, 'You are not able to go against this Philistine to fight with him, for you are but a youth, and he has been a man of war from his youth.' But David said to Saul, 'Your servant used to keep sheep for his father. And when there came a lion, or a bear, and took a lamb from the flock, I went after him and struck him and delivered it out of his mouth. And if he arose against me, I caught him by his beard and struck him and killed him. Your servant has struck down both lions and bears, and this uncircumcised Philistine shall be like one of them, for he has defied the armies of the living God.' And David said, 'The LORD who delivered me from the paw of the lion and from the paw of the bear will deliver me from the hand of this Philistine.' And Saul said to David, 'Go, and the LORD be with you'" (1 Sam 17:33–37).

"The LORD is a warrior, The LORD is his name" (Exod 15:3 NIV).

In The Trenches

1. Last week we talked about Jacob, a man who was afraid. This week we talk about David, a man who was not afraid. Read the passage. David is about to go out and fight with the giant named Goliath. Why is David not afraid? What has his experience taught him about facing fearful situations?

2. Why do you think King Saul is surprised and does not understand? Whom do you think King Saul trusts in? Read 1 Samuel 13:8–14.

Scouting the Territory

Day 2

Ever since the fall, evil has been on the earth. But thanks to social media, we are all daily witnesses to its global "bite." It is no longer something "out there," but right here, among us. And those with dragon hearts revel in our fear. They terrify. They intimidate. They are all teeth; grotesque appetites for wholesale destruction. And we feel helpless. The Bible is full of battlegrounds where God's people felt just like we do. The story of David and Goliath teaches us some important truths about ourselves and God—that what looks huge and overwhelming is not as big as it seems. And it reminds us that we need a mediator, a worthy dragon slayer, when facing battles with dragons.

In 1 Samuel 17, David is the kid brother sent to the battle front, to bring supplies and provisions to his older brothers, who are soldiers in the king's army. He is definitely not the little kid of Sunday school fame. But he is also not yet twenty years of age, as Numbers 1:45 refers to those who are twenty and older as countable for the army and able to go to war. He is also likely a well-built and powerful young man. He claims to have successfully wrestled and killed a bear and a lion in his role as shepherd. This is no shrimp. But there is also more to him than his appearance. He not only looks like a warrior, but he has a warrior's heart.

He arrives in camp just in time for the daily blast of fear from the opposition's elite weapon—the giant, Goliath. According to the ESV notes, Goliath was about nine feet, nine inches tall, an obviously broad-chested warrior who wore a 125 pound coat of armor with ease, and who had been strutting arrogantly in front of the army of Israel for forty days, taunting with words while threatening everyone with a fifteen pound iron spearhead attached to a shaft that was "like a weaver's beam."[1] He had been daring Israel to send out a champion to fight him. Clearly no one in Israel had someone of his magnitude to offer in combat. It states in 1 Samuel 17:11 that from King Saul down to the lowest soldier in the ranks, all were "dismayed and greatly afraid." And this made Goliath all the more arrogant.

1. ESV study notes, 519.

"Am I not a Philistine?" he asked. "Are you not servants of Saul?" (1 Sam 17:8 ESV) "Just send out your champion," he seems to imply, "and whoever wins, wins all." All Israel is thinking is, "how can we possibly survive this?"

But David sees the world differently. The nation of Israel is not primarily the servant of King Saul. They are the servants of the living God. David asks, "Who is this uncircumcised Philistine that he should defy the armies of the living God?" (1 Sam 17:26) Have you forgotten to whom you belong? Have you forgotten what kind of God you serve? We fear because we know we are inadequate for the task, and therefore overwhelmed by the enemy. We fear man when we should fear God. "The fear of the LORD is the beginning of wisdom" (Prov 9:10a). "The fear of the LORD leads to life; then one rests content, untouched by trouble" (Prov 19:23). When we fear God first, we see our situation more clearly. It looks dire because it is dire. It is dire because we cannot fix it ourselves. Because we cannot fix it ourselves, we are dependent on the one who can change everything with a word. "So shall my word be that goes out from my mouth; it shall not return to me empty, but it shall accomplish that which I purpose, and shall succeed in the thing for which I sent it" (Isa 55:11). All God needs is a word! And we have a long history of his rescue, his redemption, his power. "See now that I, even I, am he, and there is no god besides me; I kill and I make alive; I wound and I heal; and there is none that can deliver out of my hand" (Deut 32:39). There it is in the song of Moses, the song Israel was commanded to sing in perpetuity. Remember who you serve. Remind yourself of what God can do, what he has done for you. He rescued you from Pharaoh. He redeemed you with blood from the death of the firstborn. He took care of you in the wilderness. He was your warrior king when you conquered the Promised Land. Why are you afraid?

Why are we afraid? Because, like Jesus' disciples in the New Testament, the waves in our storm are enormous and intimidating (Matt 8:23–27; Mark 4:35–41; Luke 8:22–25). Because like Peter, we are afraid of being singled out, noticed before the watching and condemning world as one connected to the man on the cross (Matt 26:69–75; Mark 14:66–72; Luke 22:55–62; John 18:15–18). We are afraid because we desire peace and safety, and our own little universe is a dangerous place.

But we weren't intended to control our universe; not even a world full of hungry, destructive dragons. Christ is the Dragon Slayer. He fought for our redemption with his own blood. He rose from the dead to conquer death. He stands at the right hand of the Father in heaven to intercede on our behalf. The Holy Spirit fights daily for us against our own sinful natures. He will fight alongside us to the end as we struggle and stumble through the trials and tests of this life.

God gave Israel a great warrior—David, who fought for Israel. But David is not the ultimate warrior king. He understood how much he depended on God to fight his battles. He trusted God, the true Warrior King, to stand with him, to fight alongside him, and to bring victory. And Goliath went down with a rock and a sling—a glorious picture to Israel and to us about who is really in charge.

It is not about us. It has never been about us. It has always been, and will always be about the great Dragon Slayer, the God of the universe. The Lord is our warrior. The Lord is his name. And just as David asked Israel, Jesus continues to challenge us, "Why are you afraid, O you of little faith?" (Matt 8:26).

In The Trenches

1. What kind of dragons are in your life?

2. Why is it important to look to Christ when facing the dragons in your life?

3. What is good fear? How does having good fear help us to better fight dragons?

Day 3

Studying the Battle Plan

"Why should the nations say,
'Where is their God?'
Our God is in the heavens;
he does all that he pleases.

Their idols are silver and gold,
the work of human hands.
They have mouths, but do not speak;
eyes, but do not see.
They have ears, but do not hear,

noses, but do not smell.
They have hands, but do not feel:
feet, but do not walk;
and they do not make a sound in their throat.
Those who make them become like them;
so do all who trust in them.

O Israel, trust in the LORD!
He is their help and their shield.
O house of Aaron, trust in the LORD!
He is their help and their shield.
You who fear the LORD, trust in the LORD!
He is their help and their shield" (Ps 115:2–11).

In The Trenches

1. What does this psalm teach us about trust and worship?
2. What does it tell us about idols?

Day 4

I Love My Shoes—A Dialogue with Idols

I love the way
the raindrops play a tin roof,
Music on a steely drum,
Glorious rhythm,
Dancing in a world of gray.

I love the chattering of birds
that fill a million crevices with song,
Swelling layers upon layering of praise
that call the sun,
And start the day.

I love the sky
In clouds,

In streaks of color,
All its vastness
covering the world below,
With moving shadows,
Glinting light.
A living canopy of wind,
Of still,
Of cold and wet,
Of raging storm,
Of blazing warm,
Of brilliant bright.

I love the earth,
The sky,
The seas.
Do you love Me more than these?

I love the people in my life,
The man who lays beside me
in my bed at night,
My gentle husband,
Friend and lover,
Tuned together over time,
In many struggles
bound to know and love each other
as we are.
I love the babies we have made,
Our babies' babies,
All the family that bloomed
when two are one.

I love the mother,
Father,
Sister,
Brother,
Family extending far beyond
our home and hearth to fill a church.

I love community and neighbor,
Friendships labored
out of life and prayer,
Pledged to favor side by side
in celebrations and disease.
Do you love Me more than these?

I love the things that fill a life,
That decorate
the way I spend,
My hungry closet filled with clothes to wear.
The shelves of books,
The music anytime I
care to hear.
Heat or air as I demand,
Flushing toilets,
Showers,
Water under my command.
Certainly a world of grace,
His gifts to me,
His love has made this generous ease.
Do you love Me more than these?

I love my shoes.

In The Trenches

1. What does God keep asking the speaker?
2. Are the things she loves good things?
3. What is she struggling with?

Day 5

Heart Check

1. Read Isaiah 44:6.

2. Whom should I fear? Whom should I trust?

3. Is there anything or anyone that can do what God can do?

4. What has God promised to do?

Week 13—Hearts of Shechem

Day 1

Studying the Battle Plan

"Abram passed through the land to the place at Shechem, to the oak of Moreh. At that time the Canaanites were in the land. Then the LORD appeared to Abram and said, 'To your offspring I will give this land.' So he built there an altar to the Lord, who had appeared to him" (Gen 12:6–7).

"And all who went out of the gate of his city listened to Hamor and his son Shechem, and every male was circumcised, all who went out of the gate of his city. On the third day, when they were sore, two of the sons of Jacob, Simeon and Levi, Dinah's brothers, took their swords and came against the city while it felt secure and killed all the males. They killed Hamor and his son Shechem with the sword and took Dinah out of Shechem's house and went away. The sons of Jacob came upon the slain and plundered the city, because they had defiled their sister" (Gen 34:24–27).

"As to the rest of the Kohathites belonging to the Kohathite clans of the Levites, the cities allotted to them were out of the tribe of Ephraim. To them were given Shechem, the city of refuge for the manslayer, with its pasturelands in the hill country of Ephraim, Gezer with its pasturelands" (Josh 21:20–21).

In The Trenches

1. This week is about a place as much as about people. Shechem, and its surrounding area has been around for thousands of years. Located in central Israel, people have passed through this area on their way to somewhere else. It is the ultimate public highway. Geographically positioned, Shechem is a perfect picture of the spiritual battleground that has existed since Genesis 3 between God and The Dragon. All through the Bible, the question is, "Who owns the hearts of Shechem?" Is it a place for God's people or is it dragon territory?

2. In the three short passages given, when are the people honoring God and when are they all about dragons?

Day 2

Scouting the Territory

Some places just seem to attract conflict. The American state of Kentucky is one of those places. During the American Civil War, the Kentucky state government declared itself loyal to the Union, but the State Guard, made up of seasoned volunteer militia groups, supported the South. According to the Kentucky National Guard website, 40,000 men fought for the Confederacy, and 100,000 men were allied with the Union.[1] Northern sections of the state were bloody battlegrounds. All dragon wars lead to death, but some are merely skirmishes; one dragon raging against another for control of its hoard. Choosing sides, whether North or South, likely included a clouded mix of motivations ranging from noble ideals to self-aggrandizing passions for the hoard. But such is the complexity of human hearts; hearts at war with themselves and with each other. And here we have the core of all dragon wars—the heart. Who owns the heart, The Dragon or the King? Shechem and its surrounding valley is a battlefield in the war for hearts.

The ESV study notes on Joshua 24 comment that "the archaeological record demonstrates that the city of Shechem was an important center of pagan worship in the Middle Bronze Age (2100–1550 BC)."[2] Dragon terri-

---

1. Kentucky National Guard, "From a Time of Peace."
2. ESV study notes, 429.

tory! Yet our first biblical recorded event in Shechem is Abram arriving in Canaan from Ur, hearing God's promise of the land, and building an altar to worship the Lord. And so the battle begins. Who will own the hearts in Shechem? With the rape of Jacob's daughter Dinah, and the horrifying deception and deadly retaliation by her brothers, Simeon and Levi, (Genesis 34) the score is one for the dark side. Then amazingly, when the Israelites arrive hundreds of years later to take possession of the promised land, the land of murdered Shechemites becomes the Levite city of refuge for manslayers. Mercy and grace have conquered.

One of the most dramatic scenes played out in the valley of Shechem was the covenant renewal ceremony proscribed in Deuteronomy 27, and played out in Joshua 8. It is a graphic picture of the very war at stake. Half of the tribes of Israel were instructed to stand on top of Mount Gerizim and shout out God's covenant blessings, while the other half were told to stand on Mount Ebal and shout out God's covenant curses as a sign of their covenant fidelity as they came into the land of promise. One can almost hear the echoes of God's law reverberating up and down the valley. At the end of the conquest, Joshua made a final covenant renewal charge to the nation of Israel at Shechem, where he first, and then all the people, vowed to serve the Lord alone, to reaffirm their commitment to complete obedience.

I would like to be able to say both these ceremonies made a major difference in cementing Israelite loyalties to the Lord, and that the hearts of God's people truly belonged to him. But Judges 8 and 9 show Israel faithless. Such is the nature of dragon wars; hearts wandering, hearts easily drawn away to other lovers. Judges 8 tells us that God's people had traded their worship of him for worship of Baal. And out of this betrayal came a fierce succession of dragon wars and dragon kings over the long and sordid history of Israel.

In The Trenches

1. Read Deuteronomy 27:1–26; 28:1–14; 30:19–20. What is at stake for God's people?

2. Read Deuteronomy 4:25–31. What does God say about the battleground of people's hearts? What should give us hope? How can God offer us hope?

Day 3

Scouting the Territory

I will only highlight three dragon kings from this area. The first was Abimelech, the son of Gideon. He showed his dragon heart when he called out curses from Mount Gerizim; the mountain God had ordained for shouting out blessings. His solution to gaining hearts was to kill his seventy brothers—contenders for a throne that was of his own making. He was merciless, cruel, and vindictive, known only for betrayal and blood. Murder and death followed him everywhere he went. He was mortally wounded when a woman pushed a millstone over the top of a tower onto his head.

The second dragon king, Rehoboam, rightful successor to King Solomon, tried to set up his kingdom in Shechem. But he, too, had a dragon heart. He ruled with arrogance, with an iron fist, with hard labor, and without grace. He ended up fleeing to Jerusalem as Jeroboam (dragon king number three), the son of one of Solomon's servants, rose up to take his place. The prophet, Ahijah, had told Jeroboam that he would rule ten of the twelve tribes, taking away the great united kingdom of Solomon from Rehoboam, because Solomon had not kept covenant with the Lord. But Ahijah also reminded Jeroboam that his right to those ten tribes, the northern kingdom of Israel, was conditional on Jeroboam's obedience to God. Jeroboam fortified Shechem as one of his favored cities. But he also chose the dragon path, setting up two new places of worship, one at Dan and one at Bethel, and made golden calves for each. He even created feasts to go with his false worship and swiftly carried a whole portion of Israel into institutionalized apostasy. In the rest of the history of Israel, worshipping false gods was referred to as "the sin of Jeroboam." What a legacy! The ten northern tribes, after years and years of idolatry, were finally destroyed by the Assyrians, and these tribes never returned to the land. They disappeared altogether. The Assyrians brought a hodgepodge of their own captives into Canaan to repopulate the land. And 2 Kings 17:25 tells us that the Lord sent devouring lions in among them because none of the new inhabitants worshiped the true God. Apostate priests of Israel, who had previously been captured, were sent back to the land to teach the people "the law of the god of the land" (2 Kgs 17:26). It would seem that the dragons had won decisively. Northern Israel became Samaria, an amalgamation of religious

83

ideas dressed in a faintly Jewish overcoat. What could generations of idol worshipers tell anyone about the true King of the universe?

But this is where the story gets the most interesting. Fast forward to the first century AD, and a small village in Samaria, called Sychar. Sychar is thought to be the old name for Askar, less than a mile from Jacob's well, and on the slope of Mount Ebal. Jacob's well is believed to have been located in Shechem.[3] So we are back to where we started. Only this time, we come face to face with the Dragon Slayer, the creator of the universe, and he is in conversation with a woman at the well. Underneath this seemingly casual conversation, a battle is raging for the heart of this woman. Jesus speaks eternal truth: "Everyone who drinks of this water will be thirsty again, but whoever drinks of the water that I will give him will never be thirsty again" (John 4:13). The Creator is divining the heart: "You are right in saying, 'I have no husband'; for you have had five husbands, and the one you now have is not your husband" (John 4:17b–18). The Creator is revealing his glory: "God is spirit, and those who worship him must worship in spirit and truth. The woman said to him, 'I know that Messiah is coming (he who is called Christ). When he comes, he will tell us all things.' Jesus said to her, 'I who speak to you am he'" (John 4:24–26).

What happens to hearts when the Dragon Slayer enters in? "Many Samaritans from that town believed in him because of the woman's testimony, 'He told me all that I ever did.' So when the Samaritans came to him, they asked him to stay with them, and he stayed there two days. And many more believed because of his word. They said to the woman, 'It is no longer because of what you said that we believe, for we have heard for ourselves, and we know that this is indeed the Savior of the world'" (John 4:39–42). The Slayer's words alone can undo The Dragon's power. Shechem, Mount Ebal, and Mount Gerazim, will never be the same, as the word of God, and the grace of God reverberate once again up and down the valley.

The Slayer's presence will demand war. He will not fight The Dragon here, but nearby, outside the city walls of Jerusalem. He does not do it with a sword, but with a sacrifice. He will let God the Father rain Mt. Ebal's curses on him. He will take them all, swallow them, absorb them, destroy them. He will be our bloody ground, our death. And then, he will rise from the dead, so that people in Shechem, people in Jerusalem, people from every corner of the world will be able to wrest their hearts away from dragon thoughts, from dragon hoards, and walk away from the mortally wounded

3. ESV study notes, 2027.

dragon forever. Shechem, like many places around the globe, has a history written in blood, but so does the Dragon Slayer. Only his bloody ground is different. His blood saves. His blood kills dragons.

In The Trenches

1. All people have dragon hearts. And yet God is a rescuer of the dragon hearted. How do we know God is greater than The Dragon or any dragon hearted person?

2. Read Ephesians 2:1–10. How does this passage match up with the Deuteronomy 4:25–31 passage we read yesterday?

Day 4

Truly Real

They all were flat,
Rice-paper thin.
Like paper dolls,
Where Self had grown too large
to shape a soul,
Where fear of feeling pain
or inconvenience,
Firmly folded lives to two dimensional displays.
Too aimless,
Flitting back and forth through air,
And they,
Potential detritus,
Danced like bits of paper
blown by every wind of doctrine,
All too easily thrown away,
Too lost in private feelings,
All too flat to find
the truth of Truly Real.

For Truly Real might tether
pain to life,

Or suffering
uncover caring's face,
At least a taste beyond the Self.

To see the Other,
Or, perhaps,
To catch a passing glance,
A chance to measure out
the edge of Whole instead of Flat—
It might make restless wispy paper
into shape and soul,
A three dimensional restore.

If only wisdom
loved impatience more,
Or thrived on selfishness and scorn.

Too late.
The danger here is shapes grotesque
if sorrow takes a bitter turn.
If only tests and trials could be better worn.

It is that fourth dimension,
That intangible,
The Holy One intruding,
Making all the difference.
Bridging us
between our flattened selves
and all the shapes and forms of Real.

Without His grand perspective,
Or His steel,
How could the Paper Thin
become much sturdier,
Unbending in the wind,
Could bear the weight of pain
or bury sin,
Could finally survive themselves,
And safely touch the sharpening thorns of

Beauty,
Truth,
And love,
Could feel these wounds and not be torn?

In The Trenches

1. This poem is filled with metaphors, pictures of the differences between dragon people and God's people. It compares dragon people to paper dolls, people whose lives are so empty it is as if they are as thin as pieces of paper. What makes people paper-doll-thin people?

2. Notice the poem also talks about suffering, about being hurt. It implies that paper thin people get uglier and more horrible when they are hurt. But real people become more real and stronger when they face suffering. Look at the last two stanzas. Who makes us into real people? What did Christ have to do to make us real?

Day 5

Heart Check

"And he said, 'Listen, all Judah and inhabitants of Jerusalem and King Jehoshaphat: Thus says the LORD to you, "Do not be afraid and do not be dismayed at this great horde, for the battle is not yours but God's."' (2 Chr 20:15)

This isn't the only time God had to remind his people that he was actually in control of the situation. There are two key phrases here: *Do not be afraid*, and *the battle is not yours but God's*. When you are in the battle, remind yourself of this.

Counter Offensive

"I saw Satan fall like lightning from heaven" (Luke 10:18).

Week 14—Born to Die

Day 1

Studying the Battle Plan

"He [Christ] entered once for all into the holy places, not by means of the blood of goats and calves but by means of his own blood, thus securing an eternal redemption" (Heb 9:12).

In The Trenches

1. Read Exodus 29. What is required for just the priests to be clean enough to serve God and his people in the temple?
2. What does this say about the holiness of God?
3. What and who is needed to end the war between us and a holy God?

Day 2

Scouting the Territory

Imagine you are an ancient Israelite, a pious follower of God. You have been cross and quarrelsome with your elderly mother all day. You didn't mean to be this cross, but now there is no peace in your home. You have confessed your sin to her. Now you must confess your sin to God. In breaking fellowship with your mother, you have also broken fellowship with your creator and covenant Lord. I don't know if we moderns fully recognize this subtle connection. To sin against your neighbor is to also sin against God. There must be atonement, restitution before a holy God. Just saying you are sorry is not enough.

Is the consequence of sin that bad? The answer: Yes. It requires a death. Someone or something must die. You choose a female lamb or goat that has no blemishes and take the animal to the entrance of the tent of meeting. The priest accepts your animal. You lay your hand on the animal's head and confess before the priest and God. "Forgive me for being unkind. I was cruel to her. Forgive me. I did not honor her. Forgive me. I am sorry." Then you kill the animal at the altar. The priest captures some of the blood on his fingers and throws some against the horns of the altar, and pours the rest of the blood at the base of the altar. There is probably blood on you, and on the priest, as well as on the ground. The animal is cut into pieces: separating the meat from the fat. And the fat is burned on the altar. The priest has made an acceptable atonement before the Lord on your behalf (Lev 4:27–35). You "murdered" your mother with your anger and your words (Matt 5:21–26), and the innocent animal has died in your place because you wouldn't hold your tongue.

Imagine a lifetime of sacrifice after sacrifice; always working to keep the slate clean between you and God; the blood running down the base of the altar into the dirt, coloring the ground and your life with the smell of animals and death. The stench is everywhere. The air is a constant smoky haze of burning carcass and consuming fire that never ends. And if you are a person with a sensitive conscience, you might be asking, "How many animals must die for me? Is it enough?"

The answer, of course, is, "No." It is never enough, because this animal can only cover this sin, this day. You will sin tomorrow. God is holy. You are not. The dragon lives on.

The word redeemer used in Job 19:25—"I know that my Redeemer lives"—is the Hebrew word, *goel*, meaning kinsman redeemer. In ancient Israel, the kinsman redeemer was a relative called to rescue another family member who could not save themselves. He could redeem property that had been sold due to debt (Lev 25:25). He could redeem a relative sold into slavery for debts due (Lev 25:47–48). He could legally avenge a murdered relative (Num 35:19). He could provide a son, an heir, to a barren widow; thus protecting the line of inheritance and blessing.

But it is here that the ancient Job identifies the solution. There needs to be a mediator between the most holy and the most unholy. And his yearning for reconciliation with God comes back to Job in 19:23–26—"Oh that my words were written! Oh that they were inscribed in a book! Oh that with an iron pen and lead they were engraved in the rock forever! For I know that my Redeemer lives, and at the last he will stand upon the earth. And after my skin has been thus destroyed, yet in my flesh I shall see God."

The dragon will die. God, through Christ, has chosen to be the lamb in your place. Christ is the Redeemer. He acts as the kinsman redeemer, or champion that stands for you when you cannot stand for yourself. Blood must be shed, and he will be the sacrifice, the last and ultimate lamb. The Slayer will be slain. "It is finished," Jesus says on the cross. It is done. No more blood. No more deaths. This is the wonder of the incarnation, of God with us. It is beyond comprehension that God can become man, be one of us. It is intensely and gravely sobering that our sin requires such a response, and that he who was born in a manger, was born to die.

In The Trenches

1. What kind of mediator do sinful, dragonish people need?

2. Why is the cross necessary?

Day 3

Postings from the Front

"For whatever reason God chose to make man as he is—limited and suffering and subject to sorrows and death—he [God] had the honesty and the courage to take his own medicine. Whatever game he is playing with his creation, he has kept his own rules and played fair. He can exact nothing from man that he has not exacted from himself. He has himself gone through the whole of human experience, from the trivial irritations of family life and the cramping restrictions of hard work and lack of money to the worst horrors of pain and humiliation, defeat, despair, and death. When he was a man, he played the man. He was born in poverty and died in disgrace and thought it well worthwhile . . . "The people who hanged Christ never, to do them justice, accused him of being a bore—on the contrary, they thought him too dynamic to be safe . . . To those who knew him, however, he in no way suggests a milk–and–water person; they objected to him as a dangerous firebrand . . . He went to parties in disreputable company and was looked upon as a 'gluttonous man and a winebibber, a friend of publicans and sinners'; he assaulted indignant tradesmen and threw them and their belongings out of the temple; he drove a coach–and–horses through a number of sacrosanct and hoary regulations; he cured diseases by any means that came handy, with a shocking casualness in the matter of other people's pigs and property . . . when confronted with neat dialectical traps, he displayed a paradoxical humor that affronted serious–minded people, and he retorted by asking disagreeably searching questions that could not be answered by rule of thumb. He was emphatically not a dull man in his human lifetime, and if he was God, there can be nothing dull about God either. But he had 'a daily beauty in his life that made us ugly', and officialdom felt that the established order of things would be more secure without him. So they did away with God in the name of peace and quietness."—Dorothy Sayers.[1]

"The day's work had ended; the tools were being counted, as usual. As the party was about to be dismissed, the Japanese guard shouted that a shovel was missing. He insisted that someone had stolen it to sell to the Thais. Striding up and down before the men, he ranted and denounced them for their wickedness . . . Screaming in broken English, he demanded that the guilty one step forward to take his punishment. No one moved; the guard's rage reached new heights of violence.

'All die! All die!' he shrieked.

To show that he meant what he said, he cocked his rifle, put it to his shoulder and looked down the sights, ready to fire at the first man at the end of them. At that moment the Argyll stepped forward, stood stiffly to attention, and said calmly, 'I did it.'

The guard unleashed all his whipped–up hate; he kicked the helpless prisoner and beat him with his fists. Still the Argyll stood rigidly to attention, with the blood streaming down his face. His silence goaded the guard to an excess of rage. Seizing his rifle by the barrel, he lifted it high over his head and, with a final howl, brought it down on the skull of the Argyll, who sank limply to the ground and did not move. Although it was perfectly clear that he

1. Sayers, *Letters to a Diminished Church*, 2, 4–5.

was dead, the guard continued to beat him and stopped only when exhausted . . . When the tools were counted again at the guard-house no shovel was missing . . . I was beginning to see that life was infinitely more complex, and at the same time more wonderful, than I had ever imagined. True, there was hatred. But there was also love. There was death. But there was also life. God had not left us. He was with us, calling us to live the divine life in fellowship. I was beginning to be aware of the miracle that God was working in the Death Camp by the River Kwai."—Ernest Gordon[2]

In The Trenches

1. Why was Jesus willing to die in disgrace? Why was this important?

2. The death camp by the River Kwai changed the day the Argyll died. People who had not cared for each other and were just trying to survive started paying attention to each other and caring for each other. Why would his death make such a difference to people who were barely surviving themselves?

Day 4

Love

Angels,
Watching from eternity
where Love resides,
Are stunned as Deity collides
with Time and Man.

Such intersection
breaks the barriers of sound,
of space.
And all Creation,
Bending,
Kneeling before Glory's face,
Can't comprehend,

2. Gordon, *To End All Wars*, 101–2, 110.

Can't understand
why Holy would descend
to be with Man,
Or why the one receiving
such amazing condescension
turns away.

A snub.
So royally offensive!

Why would He Who Knew,
Still love,
Still eagerly pursue,
Still offer grace,
A grace erasing all the petty vanities,
The gross idolatries
that Man displays,
A grace of blood,
A grace to death,
A sacrifice,
Where He Who Knew
Drinks all God's Holy wrath
to take Man's place?

In The Trenches

1. What does the poem tell us real love looks like?

2. Read 1 John 4:19; 2 Corinthians 5:14–15; Galatians 5:13–15, 22–24. Whom do we love? Why do we love? How can we love? What does real love look like in us?

Day 5

Heart Check

1. Read Isaiah 53:5.

2. This is the end game in the great battle between us and the Dragon. Jesus was spit upon, he was tortured, he was stripped and shamed, he was scourged and beaten, he was crucified. To the world, this is a hopeless, horrific defeat. To God and to us, this is the ultimate conquest. Think about it. Revel in it. Praise God for his lavish gift of love to you and to me.

Week 15—Come Lord Jesus

Day 1

Studying the Battle Plan

"But now in Christ Jesus you who once were far off have been brought near by the blood of Christ. For he himself is our peace, who has made us both one and has broken down in his flesh the dividing wall of hostility by abolishing the law of commandments expressed in ordinances, that he might create in himself one new man in place of the two, so making peace, and might reconcile us both to God in one body through the cross, thereby killing the hostility" (Eph 2:13–17).

In The Trenches

1. How are we to respond to God's merciful and gracious love for us?
2. Read 1 Corinthians 15:49; Ephesians 4:24. What does it mean to become a new man?

Day 2

Heaven Comes

Heaven comes.
The radiance of Holy Glory comes,
Intruding into womb,
His vast eternity

Waiting,
Cloistered,
Growing in our darkness,
Pushing,
Groaning into time.

How can the One who made the hay,
Who holds the manger
(Dirt, saliva,
All its parts together,
Mixed with blood,
Placenta),
choose our tomb,
A forlorn place to lay His head?

Why does Emmanuel,
God with us,
Make wrapping burial cloths and caves
His earthly bed?

He comes.
Because intruding
pushes back against our Grave,
That darkness relishing the scars of war.

Where else but in our darkness
Would this Light descend?
Where else would God descend
But into skin?
Where else but deity in skin
Could swallow all the sin that we adore.
Where else but all our sin on Him
Could crush His Holy Life,
And in that crushing,
All the rage of stones and mausoleums,
Urns and ashes,
Shudder,
Fall before His Cosmic Throne.

The Dig

Idols,
Idols everywhere.

Like ancient ruins,
Tumbled rocks,
And toppled stones,
The careless thrones for other gods
strewn back and forth across my path,
A tell to my rebellion
scattered on my heart.
And every thought
Might resurrect,
Or recognize these eyeless tombs,
If not for Him who clears a path.

Relentlessly,
My Archaeologist is digging up,
Unearthing death,
Identifying,
Tagging,
Then removing obstacles,
My obstacles,
The cherished friends of my hypocrisy.
Where would I be
if He was not among the tombs?

In The Trenches

1. Read two short poems today: "The Dig," and "Heaven Comes." Each poem talks about the different ways that belonging to Christ changes our lives.

2. What is Christ doing to our thinking, attitudes, and actions?

3. How does Christ change the way we die? What has happened to death?

Day 3

Postings from the Front

"'Then the lion said—but I [Eustace] don't know if it spoke —"You will have to let me undress you." I was afraid of his claws, I can tell you, but I was pretty nearly desperate now. So I just lay flat down on my back to let him do it. The very first tear he made was so deep that I thought it had gone right into my heart. And when he began pulling the skin off, it hurt worse than anything I've ever felt. The only thing that made me able to bear it was just the pleasure of feeling the stuff peel off. You know—if you've ever picked the scab of a sore place. It hurts like billy-oh but it is such fun to see it coming away.'

'I know exactly what you mean,' said Edmund.

'Well, he peeled the beastly stuff right off—just as I thought I'd done it myself the other three times, only they hadn't hurt—and there it was lying on the grass: only ever so much thicker, and darker, and more knobbly–looking than the others had been. And there was I as smooth and soft as a peeled switch and smaller than I had been. Then he caught hold of me—I didn't like that much for I was very tender underneath now that I'd no skin on—and threw me into the water. It smarted like anything but only for a moment. After that it became perfectly delicious and as soon as I started swimming and splashing I found that all the pain had gone from my arm. And then I saw why. I'd turned into a boy again."'—C.S. Lewis. [1]

In The Trenches

1. Remember when Eustace had been turned into a dragon? Well, now he tells Edmund how Aslan changed him back into a boy. In the Narnia books, C.S. Lewis writes pretend stories to teach real truth. What real truths can we learn from this story? Can Eustace make himself back into a boy? Was it comfortable becoming a boy again?

1. Lewis, *Dawn Treader*, 108–9.

2. If you have read *The Voyage of the Dawn Treader*, you know that Eustace becomes a kinder, more caring boy after this. How is his experience like becoming a new man?

Day 4

"And sometimes they sacrificed to the old stone gods,
Made heathen vows, hoping for Hell's
Support, the Devil's guidance in driving
Their affliction off. That was their way,
And the heathen's only hope, Hell
Always in their hearts, knowing neither God
Nor His passing as He walks through our world,
the Lord.
Of Heaven and earth; their ears could not hear
His praise nor know His glory. Let them
Beware, those who are thrust into danger,
Clutched at by trouble, yet can carry no solace
In their hearts, cannot hope to be better! Hail
To those who will rise to God, drop off
Their dead bodies and seek our Father's peace!"
—*Beowulf*[2]

In The Trenches

1. *Beowulf* is a very old medieval epic poem about a dragon slayer. How does the speaker let us know that many of the people in the story have dragonish hearts?

2. What does the speaker encourage those people to do?

2. Raffel, *Beowulf*, lines 175–88, 9–10.

Day 5

Heart Check

1. Read Psalm 103:10–12.

2. Do you truly believe you are loved and forgiven, every day, every hour? Practice keeping "short accounts." Take your sinful thoughts and deeds to God as soon as possible. Thank him for his gracious love and mercy. Your sin was paid for. It was covered at the cross. Ask him to help you "bury it," to let go, and start again. Some days may seem like a relentless passion of asking forgiveness. So be it. His was a relentless passion of love in action for you.

Week 16—Born to Live

Day 1

Studying the Battle Plan

"But when the fullness of time had come, God sent forth his Son, born of woman, born under the law, to redeem those who were under the law, so that we might receive adoption as sons. And because you are sons, God has sent the Spirit of his Son into our hearts, crying, 'Abba! Father!' So you are no longer a slave, but a son, and if a son, then an heir through God" (Gal 4:4–7).

In The Trenches

1. These verses describe our Dragon Slayer. How many of his attributes can you identify?
2. How does Christ's coming to earth change our relationship with God?

Day 2

Emmanuel

We who stood at Sinai,
Bowed in fear,
Afraid to come too close
before the dark,
The thunderclouds of Holiness,

In abject terror of our death.

We should be still,
Be quiet,
Lost in awe,
Without a word to speak
before the miracle of Incarnation,
God becoming one of us.

How dare we speak,
When God's own army
Shouted out,
"Glory to God in the Highest!"
And we,
Fell down,
While angels filled up all the earthly air
with Heaven's throne?

I see it now.
I am alone,
Undone,
Unspeakable,
Unknowable
before such Holy Things.

But He who makes by fiat—
Word becoming flesh—
He speaks.
He comes.
He tabernacles through a womb.
Not tent,
Not temple made of stone,
But womb,
An entrance born of blood and pain,
Of suffering.

My alienation now is His.

We who stood at Sinai,
Bowed in fear,

Afraid to come too close,
Come closer in
To Zion's crest,
To view a Child,
To see a Man nailed to a Cross,
To touch His resurrection scars,
To know at last
That death itself
becomes undone,
Unspeakable.
And I—imperishable,
have I AM written on my hands.
I am the LORD's.

I see it now.
I am His own.

In The Trenches

1. Read Exodus 19:9–20 and Hebrews 12:18–24. Both of these passages talk about meeting God. Both see that meeting in terms of Mount Sinai. What made the difference between the people of the Exodus, and the people hearing the book of Hebrews?

2. Emmanuel means, "God with us." How does the speaker of the poem feel coming before a holy God?

   How does Emmanuel change the speaker's perspective? How does Emmanuel change his heart?

Day 3

Read Psalm 121; John 16:33; Romans 7:21–25; and 1 Peter 5:6–11.

In The Trenches

1. What can it mean to be a follower of Christ?

2. These Scriptures remind us that some dragons are outside of us, and some dragons are in our own hearts.

3. We do not need to fear The Dragon. How do we fight against him? Where does our strength come from?

Day 4

Scouting the Territory

I have a dear friend who is a strong Christian. She came into her relationship with Christ later in life. Her husband and grown children are not on the same page. As far as they can see, it is okay for her to go to church every week and attend Bible study, because religious people are like that. But they do not see how it should affect the rest of their lives together. Her faith has been criticized, and seen as an obstacle. Without doing anything but just being a believer, she has become an offense. There is a spiritual wall that separates her from her husband and children. She does not always handle family interactions well, but she has a humble and teachable heart; one that God is using to speak peace into her messy domestic life.

The Incarnation is about speaking peace into a messy world. What could possibly offend anyone about a manger scene—a baby asleep in an animal food trough, the vigilant and adoring parents looking on, and perhaps a shepherd or two in the wings? The offense is in the intentional intrusion of God into our mess. It is not the pretty and serene manger we see portrayed. He is not just an adorable baby waiting for the shepherds and eventual Magi. He is the I AM, the covenant–keeping God on a faithful mission of rescue to a people who do not want him. From the beginning there are those who want him dead. Because of who he is, he offends Herod to the point that this God/Man child must be hustled off to Egypt while Herod kills all the baby boys in town.

God in Christ chose to live like us; to get tired, to face sorrow, to bleed. And he continues to be intrusive all over the place. He is not interested in our excuses. He asks pointed questions that put us on the spot. He expects to be taken seriously. If you think it is right and proper to go to church, but not necessary to believe, he makes you uncomfortable. He gives equal weight to thoughts and attitudes as he does to actions. You've been exposed. Better for everyone to think how spiritually adept you are than notice how truly shallow and numbingly repetitive your spiritual life really is. You would rather not admit that you have been caught worshipping yourself.

If you despise the church and laugh at the discomfiture and hypocrisy of your religious neighbor, Jesus awakens you to the realization that you are just a different style of worshiper. There is a hole in your universe that beer and casual relationships can't fill. Filling your life with more of yourself only gives you more self and even more unease. You are running after wind as clearly as your church-going neighbor. No wonder the people of Jesus' day thought killing him would solve both problems.

It did, but not in the way the offended might hope. They had wanted him to change. Instead his death proved to be far greater and more amazing than they could possibly imagine. His death and resurrection changed them. Believing in him remade offended people into loving sons and inheritors. It made them children of the King. The world looks different when you are a child of the King of the universe.

So what do you do when the world, up close and personal, misunderstands and belittles what you know to be true? What do you do when your character is maligned, or your very personhood is attacked? Do what my friend does. She remembers that she is a child of the King. She has an inheritance that cannot be destroyed. Those around her may be busily accumulating stuff and prestige. The first is easily burned, the second forgotten. She is loved, has been rescued, and will be sustained by the King of the universe. His word holds her molecules together. He is the one keeping the world spinning on its axis. He knows her struggles and anxieties, and provides what she needs, every hour, every day.

So she prays for her family. They are the lost. They actually have nothing. And she, who has everything, has a glorious story to tell, a life to live before a watching and messy world.

In The Trenches

1. We do not like a messy world. We would love a world where everyone got along and nothing bad or uncomfortable ever happened. But a sinful world is a messy one. How should we respond when life is difficult?

2. What truths have your learned this week that encourage you as you deal with the hard times in your life?

Day 5

Heart Check

1. Read Jude 24–25.
2. What is God's long-term goal for your life?

Battle Ready

"In all circumstances take up the shield of faith, with which you can extinguish all the flaming darts of the evil one; and take the helmet of salvation, and the sword of the Spirit, which is the word of God, praying in the Spirit, with all prayer and supplication. To that end keep alert with all perseverance, making supplication for all the saints" (Eph 6:16–18).

Week 17—Spiritual Oxygen

Day 1

Studying the Battle Plan

"While they were bringing out the money that had been brought into the house of the LORD, Hilkiah the priest found the Book of the Law of the LORD given through Moses. Then Hilkiah answered and said to Shaphan the secretary, 'I have found the Book of the Law in the house of the LORD.' . . . Then Shaphan the secretary told the king, 'Hilkiah the priest has given me a book.' And Shaphan read from it before the king.

And when the king heard the words of the Law, he tore his clothes. And the king commanded Hilkiah, Ahikam the son of Shaphan, Abdon the son of Micah, Shaphan the secretary, and Asaiah the king's servant, saying, 'Go, inquire of the LORD for me and for those who are left in Israel and in Judah, concerning the words of the book that has been found. For great is the wrath of the LORD that is poured out on us, because our fathers have not kept the word of the LORD, to do according to all that is written in this book.'

Then the king sent and gathered together all the elders of Judah and Jerusalem. And the king went up to the house of the LORD, with all the men of Judah and the inhabitants of Jerusalem and the priests and the Levites, all the people both great and small. And he read in their hearing all the words of the Book of the Covenant that had been found in the house of the LORD. And the king stood in his place and made a covenant before the LORD, to walk after the LORD and to keep his commandments and his testimonies and his statutes, with all his heart and all his soul, to perform the words of the covenant that were written in this book. Then he made all who were present in Jerusalem and in Benjamin join in it. And the inhabitants of Jerusalem did according to the covenant of God, the God of their fathers.

So all the service of the LORD was prepared that day, to keep the Passover and to offer burnt offerings on the altar of the LORD, according to the command of King Josiah. And the people of Israel who were present kept the Passover at that time, and the Feast of Unleavened Bread seven days. No Passover like it had been kept in Israel since the days of Samuel the prophet. None of the kings of Israel had kept such a Passover as was kept by Josiah, and the priests and the Levites, and all Judah and Israel who were present, and the inhabitants of Jerusalem. In the eighteenth year of the reign of Josiah this Passover was kept" (2 Chr 34:14–15, 18–21, 29–32; 35:16–19).

In The Trenches

1. What changed the heart of the king and the people?

2. How did it change the way they lived?

Day 2

Scouting the Territory

My husband and I have been part of different communities over the years; both America's east and west coasts, as well as rural and more populated areas. Our rural experience was strong on friendship and neighbors, but weak on churches. We were members of a local church that thrived on programs and family life, but had a tenuous hold on the gospel, and we regularly listened to sermons that were more homilies than godly instruction. We attended because it was the only church in town that still taught the Bible as truth and used long–standing biblical materials for both adult and children's Sunday school. The word of God speaks even to hearts in famine, but we worshipped under thin teaching.

One weekend each month we would pack up the children, and drive the hour trip to my parents for family fun and refreshment. While on the road, we would inevitably pick up a powerful gospel–centered pastor on the radio and feast on his sermon. Suddenly we would remember how hungry we were! We had forgotten, nibbling spiritual *Pablum* week after week. And hearing the word was not just food for the soul, but fresh air. Not only had we not been eating well, but the air around us was stale. The words of life would wash over us, the smell of grace would lift us up, as we breathed in clean air and let the word minister to our hearts. It was like breathing pure oxygen; heady, refreshing, filling. And being the word of God, it was also convicting. All the daily junk that had been crowding space in our lives—the worries, the arguments, the fog of our own sin—was revealed as the useless, empty stuff it was, and it was swept away as we listened.

We need oxygen to breathe. We need it to live. The word of God is our spiritual oxygen. When we don't read it, breathe it, devour it, our lives feel stale and off–centered. And life makes us tired. Israel was very tired. King Manasseh, the longest reigning king of the southern kingdom of Israel, had reigned in Judah for fifty–five years. And most of his reign was a horrifying time of terrible evils. He led the people into institutionalized idolatry, sacrificed his own children as offerings, and dealt in mediums and necromancers. At the end of his life he realized what he had done and humbled himself before the Lord. He made efforts to restore proper worship, but the damage was done. He died, leaving behind a nation of who had forgotten God, and a nasty son who only reigned for two years because of his own apostasy. Enter grandson Josiah, who began his reign at the age of eight. In the twelfth year of his reign, the Scriptures tell us he cleaned Judah's house, purging the land of idols and idolatrous practices. In the eighteenth year, he decided it was time to clean God's house. While they were repairing and restoring what had become a ruin, the Book of the Law, the word of God, was discovered in the rubble. The scroll was hurried to the king and read in his presence. Josiah breathed in its fresh, stinging air and crumpled under its convicting power. It was good to clean house, he realized, but not enough. "Hear, O Israel: The LORD our God, the LORD is one. You shall love your God with all your heart and with all your soul and with all your might. And these words that I command you today shall be on your heart" (Deut 6:4–6). Josiah tore his clothes in grief. It wasn't enough to turn behaviors, to do the right things. The heart must turn toward God as well. And the curses for disobedience were as stinging as the truth: pestilence, famine, oppression, and death. God's people were dying of spiritual hunger and in mortal danger of judgment.

Josiah consulted Huldah, the prophetess. "Thus says the LORD," she said to the king, "I will bring disaster upon this place and upon its inhabitants, all the curses that are written in the book that was read before the king of Judah" (2 Chr 34:24). But, it would not happen in his time. "Because your heart was tender and you humbled yourself before God when you heard his words against this place and its inhabitants, and you have humbled yourself before me and have torn your clothes and wept before me, I also have heard you" (2 Chr 34:27). The king gathered all the people in Jerusalem and read the scroll to them. He made all who were under his reign join with him in covenant with the Lord, "to walk after the LORD and to keep his commandments and his testimonies and his statues, with all his heart and all his soul, to perform the words of the covenant that were written in this book" (2 Chr 34:31). By the grace of God, the southern kingdom got a bracing whiff of fresh air. They heard his word. It was like breathing pure oxygen—heady, refreshing, filling, and refining. They remembered how hungry they were. They had forgotten. And the Scripture says that when they celebrated Passover, "no Passover like it had been kept in Israel since the days of Samuel the prophet. None of the kings of Israel had kept such a Passover as was kept by Josiah, and the priests and the Levites, and all Judah and Israel who were present, and the inhabitants of Jerusalem" (2 Chr 35:18). It was a glorious celebration of joy as God's promises lifted their hearts. That's what the word does. It convicts of sin. It gives us hope as it reminds us of God's love and his promises to his people.

Pick up your Bible. Read it. Meditate on his words. Let his heady oxygen fill your life.

In The Trenches

1. What did it mean to King Josiah to "clean house?"
2. What does it mean to call the Bible "spiritual oxygen?"

Day 3

Read Psalm 19:7–11; 119:11, 93, 97–105, 171–172. All of these verses are about the word of God.

In The Trenches

1. What are we commanded concerning the word?

2. What encouragement and comfort does the word of God give you?

Day 4

Fighting the Dragon

I.
Read the word,
Don't let it touch you,
Don't let it change you.
Study it
Without obedience,
Without contrition,
An academic exercise.

Whatever you do,
Don't meet the Christ,
Push back.
You might be changed,
You could have peace,
Relief from all the vagrancies of self,
Your ego tied in knots,
In vast exchanges with His Holy Rule.
Why wouldn't you want to stay the same?

It's safe,
It's so secure.
It's comfortable.
It's what I want,
It's what I know.
As long as I am king,
My rule is final.

So is death.

II.

Read the word,
Digest the word,
Underline,
Define,
Encircle it with context,
Put it on.
Put Him on.
Whatever you do,
Seek Jesus first.
Die to what I cannot change,
Die to what I cannot be
Die to me.
Hide in Him.
Forgive,
Forget,
Bear with each other patiently,
Bear trouble with humility.

I cannot see,
She does not know,
No room to carry more than what she owns,
Already burdened by humanity.
I cannot carry it alone,
But then I see
He carries me.
I did not see,
I did not know,
No room to carry more than what I own,
Already burdened by humanity.

He has already swallowed this indignity
we both are wearing,
Carrying the sins between two friends,
Absorbing what is left undone,
Already covered,
Not unloved,

Not forgotten.
Even if the rift should last into eternity,
Someday this sorrow
Will be crushed and swept away.
Whatever you do,
Seek Jesus first.

Die to what you cannot change.
Die to what you cannot be
Die to me.
Heal two souls unraveling.
Lord, set us free.

In The Trenches

1. Now we are fighting against the Dragon in earnest. What should we not do? Why is it sometimes easier to live this way?

2. What should we do? How are we able to do what is required?

Day 5

Heart Check

"Let the word of Christ dwell in you richly, teaching and admonishing one another in all wisdom, singing psalms and hymns and spiritual songs, with thankfulness in your hearts to God" (Col 3:16).

Corrie ten Boom, in her book, *The Hiding Place*, talks about her evenings in the barracks at the Nazi women's extermination camp, Ravensbruck (September 8–December 31, 1944) with her sister, Betsie:

"They were services like no others, these times in Barracks 28. A single meeting might include a recital of the Magnificat in Latin by a group of Roman Catholics, a whispered hymn by some Lutherans, and a sotto–voce chant by Eastern Orthodox women. With each moment the crowd around us would swell, packing the nearby platforms, hanging over the edges, until the high structures groaned and swayed.

At last either Betsie or I would open the Bible. Because only the Hollanders could understand the Dutch text, we would translate aloud in German. And then we would hear the life–giving words passed back along the aisles in French, Polish, Russian, Czech, back into Dutch. They were little previews of heaven, these evenings beneath the lightbulb. I would think of Harlem, each substantial church set behind its wrought–iron fence and its barrier of doctrine. And I would know again that in darkness God's truth shines most clear." [1]

1. Women died there every day. Many were starving and sick. Betsie was dying. Yet Corrie calls the word of God life–giving words. Why?

2. Why is worship of God a great weapon against dragons?

1. Ten Boom, et al., *The Hiding Place*, 212–13.

Week 18—Offensive Weapons

Day 1

Studying the Battle Plan

"In all circumstances take up the shield of faith, with which you can extinguish all the flaming darts of the evil one; and take the helmet of salvation, and the sword of the Spirit, which is the word of God, praying at all times in the Spirit, with all prayer and supplication. To that end keep alert with all perseverance, making supplication for all the saints" (Eph 6:16–18).

Day 2

Scouting the Territory

I am coming to the end of a wonderful vacation week, enjoying my children and grandchildren. It has been guaranteed noise, mess, busyness, and fun. We have toured the Grand Canyon ("Everybody needs a hand," "Stay away from the edge"), and enjoyed meals and games together. I have rocked babies, and had precious moments with toddlers, school–age kids, teenagers, and adults.

This last week was a mountain of wonder, of beauty and joy, that ended with a minor valley—one of our cars in the family caravan heading home (the one with the most children in it) broke down on the highway when we were all tired and the outside temperature was over one hundred degrees. We move back and forth in this life between the mountaintop experiences and the valleys, with our regular rhythms sandwiched in between. We are used to this tug and pull, this tension between awe in God and his incredible creation, and frustration when our world breaks down. And we are all, by nature, weak people. Exhaustion, illness, misunderstandings, emergencies, and loss are all a part of the human experience. These weaknesses wear us down, break our fellowship with family and friends, and can bring on anxiety, anger, and depression. But it can also, by the workings of the Holy Spirit, bring out our best. Struggle is one of God's favorite tools to redirect our attentions back toward him. Whether the valley is only a tiresome adventure in annoyance, or one of those dark moments that puncture our complacencies, our sense of self and security, and we feel like we can't breathe; we are called to trust, to focus ourselves and our hearts on Christ.

How do we do that? Ephesians 6:17–18 talks about two offensive weapons in our arsenal—prayer and the word of God. Prayer leans our hearts toward God, and we are to pray "at all times in the Spirit." To pray in the Spirit, according to Romans 8:26–27, is to recognize that the Holy Spirit is always interceding for us, fine-tuning our prayers into accordance with God's will, unpacking all our needs, even when all we can say is, "Jesus, help me!"

The passage from Ephesians calls the word of God, "the sword of the Spirit," given to us to keep our heads and our hearts clear. Scripture is God pouring out his heart in us. It is God speaking to us; teaching us, correcting and training our hearts and our actions so that we may be "equipped for every good work" (2 Tim 3:16–17). We need to be listening. Dragons want us to doubt God, to get lost in our feelings of the moment—our discouragements, and our fears. Christ commands us to hold on, to believe, to trust.

The early church was soundly based on three simple truths: First, that Christ died in our place to redeem us from our sin. Second, Christ rose again from the dead, conquering forever both the sin and death that enslaved us. And finally, he gave us the Holy Spirit after his ascension into heaven to instruct us, to grow us, and to guarantee God's promises to us. It was a truth so powerful that it turned ordinary fishermen into bold articulate witnesses, even to their deaths, and changed the world's history and cultures forever. It is truth we can thrive on; turning our lives, our mountains and valleys into imperfect but persistent slogs of perseverance and grace. Some days will be rich feasts of study and meditation. Other days will be leaner; bite-sized bits of Scripture like fast food, not enough to live on, but just enough to keep going. The important thing is to keep your focus on Christ, to be in a spirit of prayer about your thoughts, fears, concerns, and joys. Cultivate a daily life of fellowship with the one who calls you his beloved. Trust the Holy Spirit to give you his strength and his grace in your weakness. And above all, keep praying, keep your eyes up, and don't put down your sword.

Day 3

Postings from the Front

"In a world of created changeable things,
Christ and his Word alone remain unshaken.
O to forsake all creatures,
to rest as a stone on him the foundation,
to abide in him, be borne up by him . . .
May I always lay hold upon this mediator,
as realized object of faith,
and alone worthy by his love to bridge the gulf.
Let me know that he is dear to me by his Word;
I am one with him by the Word on his part,
and by faith on mine;
If I oppose the Word I oppose my Lord when he is most near;
If I receive the Word I receive my Lord wherein he is nigh.
O thou who hast the hearts of all men in thine hand,
form my heart according to the Word,
according to the image of thy Son,
So shall Christ the Word, and his Word, be my strength and comfort."
—*The Valley of Vision*[1]

In The Trenches

1. This is a portion of a prayer written many, many years ago. What does the writer remind himself about Christ and his word?

2. What does he pray for?

1. Bennett. *Valley of Vision*, 17.

Day 4

In The Trenches

1. Read 1 Thessalonians 5:17–18; James 5:13–20.
2. How often should we pray?
3. What Scripture passages that we have read give you the most comfort?
4. Consider sharing your concerns with each other and praying together.

Day 5

Heart Check

> "If then you have been raised with Christ, seek the things that are above, where Christ is, seated at the right hand of God. Set your minds on things that are above, not on things that are on earth. For you have died, and your life is hidden with Christ in God. When Christ who is your life appears, then you also will appear with him in glory" (Col 3:1–4).

This says two things: First, seek Christ, and think on Christ; when you get up, when you lie down, when times are good, when times are bad. The second underlines this—Christ is your life. This is a lifetime love relationship with the one who loved you first. What are practical ways you can seek Christ and think on Christ in your day–to–day living?

Week 19—Spiritual Breathing

Day 1

Studying the Battle Plan

"And when he [Herod] had seized him, he put him in prison, delivering him over to four squads of soldiers to guard him, intending after the Passover to bring him out to the people. So Peter was kept in prison, but earnest prayer for him was made to God by the church.

Now when Herod was about to bring him out, on that very night, Peter was sleeping between two soldiers, bound with two chains, and sentries before the door were guarding the prison. And behold, an angel of the Lord stood next to him, and a light shone in the cell. He struck Peter on the side and woke him, saying, 'Get up quickly.' And the chains fell off his hands. And the angel said to him, 'Dress yourself and put on your sandals.' And he did so. And he said to him, 'Wrap your cloak around you and follow me.' And he went out and followed him. He did not know that what was being done by the angel was real, but thought he was seeing a vision. When they had passed the first and the second guard, they came to the iron gate leading into the city. It opened for them of its own accord, and they went out and went along one street, and immediately the angel left him. When Peter came to himself, he said, 'Now I am sure that the Lord has sent his angel and rescued me from the hand of Herod and from all that the Jewish people were expecting.'

When he realized this, he went to the house of Mary, the mother of John whose other name was Mark, where many were gathered together and were praying. And when he knocked at the door of the gateway, a servant girl named Rhoda came to answer. Recognizing Peter's voice, in her joy she did not open the gate but ran in and reported that Peter was standing at the gate. They said to her, 'You are out of your mind.' But she kept insisting that it was so, and they kept saying, 'It is his angel!' But Peter continued knocking, and when they opened, they saw him and were amazed. But motioning to them with his hand to be silent, he described to them how the Lord had brought him out of the prison. And he said, 'Tell these things to James and to the brothers.' Then he departed and went to another place" (Acts 12:4–17).

In The Trenches

1. Here is a great story on the power of prayer! Why was it important for the church to be in earnest prayer for Peter?

2. Did Peter first believe he was being freed by the angel?

Day 2

Scouting the Territory

Prayer is one of the most underrated weapons in our arsenal. We treat it as if it's our weapon of last resort, like an extra grenade in our back pocket: "Well, at least I have this to throw. Maybe it will help." The funny thing is that God doesn't need our prayers to accomplish anything. Total sovereignty is total. But he commands us to pray, to be active participants in the war against dragons, and he uses our prayers to unpack his sovereign will. There are plenty of commands to pray—pray for your enemies and those who abuse you (Matt 5:44; Luke 6:28); pray without ceasing (1 Thess 5:17); pray for each other (Jas 5:16); be constant in prayer when you are under fire (Rom 12:12). There are also attitudes in our prayers—be steadfast in prayer with a heart of thanksgiving (Col 4:2); be persistent in our prayer and don't lose heart (Luke 18:1); and prayer may come with fasting (Luke 2:37), or singing (Acts 16:25).

And then, because we are terrible at listening, God gives us a real–life example of prayer. In Acts 12, Herod Agrippa I, grandson of Herod the Great, and always a politically astute man, sees opportunity in persecuting the growing church. He executed James, one of the sons of Zebedee, and put Peter in prison. He would have dispatched Peter as well, but the seven days of Unleavened Bread that follow Passover had begun, and an execution would have desecrated this holy celebration. Herod knew when to kill, and when to bide his time.

Peter is chained to two soldiers, while two other sentries guard the door; four hardened and alert soldiers on a three hour watch rotation. From a human perspective, Peter isn't going anywhere, except to die. But there are the words: "So Peter was kept in prison, but earnest prayer for him was made to God by the church" (Acts 12:5). God is at work through the prayers of his people. Half asleep, Peter suddenly realizes there is an angel next to him, nudging him. Peter thinks he is seeing a vision. The chains fall off his hands. The angel continues to direct him: "Dress yourself and put on your sandals. Wrap your cloak around you and follow me" (Acts 12: 8). Almost sleepwalking, Peter obeys, passing the guards and walking out through a now open iron gate into the city. The angel leaves, and Peter is fully awake now, standing alone on a dark street. The Lord has rescued him!

Here is where this true tale leaves that wonderful aura of God's power at work that accompanies so many biblical stories, and comes back down to an earth we know so well. Peter heads over to a home where he knows many are praying. He knocks. A servant girl, Rhoda, goes to answer. She sees Peter, and rushes back to tell the good news, leaving Peter still standing outside the gate on the street. Ah, comic relief. The story continues. Will those who are praying believe? Do they trust that God answers prayer? "You're crazy!" they say. "It's his angel!" But Rhoda keeps insisting, and Peter keeps knocking until they open the gate. "They saw him," the text says, "and were amazed" (Acts 12:16). Why were they amazed? Why are we?

Now I know it is true that they could have prayed in earnest for Peter's release, and Peter could have still died. His death could have been God's answer of "No." Sometimes we pray for someone to get well and they are "healed into heaven." But sometimes we pray for healing, and God graciously gives more time. We are still thinking of prayer as a last grenade.

We forget that prayer is a part of our ongoing dialogue with God. He speaks his word to us, and we respond in prayers of thanksgiving, prayers of praise, prayers of confession, prayers of supplication. Prayer can be formalized and public, private and instantaneous (Jesus, help me!), conversational as we are aware of his presence throughout our day, or communal as we gather together to bring both praise and shared petitions before him. It is active and relational; binding our hearts to him and to each other, a form of spiritual breathing. It changes us as we are in a spirit of prayer before him, and it changes others as we lift up their needs to him. Ephesians 6:18 gives us the picture of this powerful weapon—pray at all times, pray with perseverance for all the saints. Pray in the Spirit. According to John 4:23, to be in tune with the Holy Spirit is to be in a heart of worship. And Romans 8:26–27 tells us that it is the Holy Spirit who intercedes for us, bringing our prayers into accord with God's will.

Prayer isn't our last grenade. It is a first line of defense. It is powerful stuff—aligning us with the will of the Father, drawing our hearts into worship, thanksgiving, and peace (Phil 4:6–7), and knitting us together with each other in bonds of love (Phil 1:9). "The Lord is at hand," writes Paul. "Do not be anxious about anything, but in everything by prayer and supplication with thanksgiving let your requests be made known to God. And the peace of God which surpasses all understanding, will guard your hearts and your minds in Christ Jesus" (Phil 4:5b–7).

"In everything," says Paul. So stop thinking about the grenade. It's not about last resort. It is about breathing.

Pray.

In The Trenches

1. Did the people praying for Peter believe at first that Peter was really free?

2. Why is it hard for us to trust God in prayers, and believe he is listening and answering?

Day 3

In The Trenches

1. Read Romans 8:26–30.

2. How do we know we have confidence that God hears and answers our prayers?

3. How is God using our prayers for his glory and our good?

Day 4

In The Trenches

1. Read James 5:13–16.

2. What priority does James give to prayer?

Day 5

Heart Check

I am not a friend of airplanes. They get me where I need to go, but they are not my favorite mode of transportation. I don't like crowds or small spaces. I don't like to go fast. I am not fond of heights. I just described your basic plane—lots of people stuffed into a giant aluminum tube that zips among the clouds!

Sitting in my tight little seat between two total strangers, I used to pray fervently that God would keep me safe. One day it dawned on me that he is taking care of me all the time. Every day. There is no place that he is not there. God is everywhere. He holds the plane up, providing the best winds. He directs the pilots. He keeps the traffic controllers aware and alert. My prayer should not be, "Lord, keep me safe." My prayer should be, "Lord, thank you that you are surrounding this plane and its occupants. Help me to be aware of your loving presence."

The plane hasn't changed. The same things still bother me. But I have a new perspective and more peace. And he is teaching me to add another prayer: "Lord how can I reach out to the two strangers on either side of me?" Perhaps I am in this uncomfortable place for a divine appointment, an opportunity to be light and grace to someone God has put right next to me; someone who is literally rubbing shoulders with me. A plane is the only place I travel where I could be that close to a total stranger for five or more hours. Suddenly the plane is getting bigger. It is full of people looking for someone to really listen to their stories, their worries, and their joys. Perhaps being this high off the ground in a tightly packed metal tube is not so bad after all.

1. Do you pray, believing and trusting that God is right there, carrying you through whatever you are facing?

2. Is your prayer focused on his sovereign power, or your circumstances?

Week 20—A Slip of the Tongue

Day 1

Studying the Battle Plan

"Above all, keep loving one another earnestly, since love covers a multitude of sins. Show hospitality to one another without grumbling. As each has received a gift, use it to serve one another, as good stewards of God's varied grace: whoever speaks, as one who speaks oracles of God; whoever serves, as one who serves by the strength that God supplies —in order that in everything God may be glorified through Jesus Christ. To him belong glory and dominion forever and ever. Amen" (1 Pet 4:8–11).

In The Trenches

1. How are we to speak to each other?
2. What should be the goal of our speech?

Day 2

Postings from the Front

"Your patient must demand that all his own utterances are to be taken at their face value and judged simply on the actual words, while at the same time judging all his mother's utterances with the fullest and most oversensitive interpretation of the tone and the context and the suspected intention. She must be encouraged to do the same to him. Hence from every quarrel they can both go away convinced, or very nearly convinced, that they are quite innocent. You know the kind of thing: 'I simply ask her what time dinner will be and she flies into a temper.' Once this habit is well established you have the delightful situation of humans saying things with the express purpose of offending and yet having a grievance when offence is taken." —C. S. Lewis.[1]

"The moment you have a self at all, there is a possibility of putting yourself first—wanting to be the centre—wanting to be God, . . . "Pride leads to every other vice: it is the complete anti–God state of mind . . . If you want to find out how proud you are the easiest way is to ask yourself, 'How much do I dislike it when other people snub me, or refuse to take any notice of me, or shove their oar in, or patronise me, or show off?' The point is that each person's pride is in competition with everyone else's pride . . . Other vices may sometimes bring people together: you may find good fellowship and jokes and friendliness among drunken people or unchaste people. But Pride always means enmity—it *is* enmity. And not only enmity between man and man, but enmity to God."—C.S. Lewis[2]

In The Trenches

1. What does putting yourself first do to you and your relationships?

2. What happens when we misread what people say?

Day 3

Seductions

Are you listening to a dragon?
Don't believe a thing he says.
Dragons lie.

I heard one in the garden,

1. Lewis, *Screwtape Letters*, 132.
2. Lewis, *Mere Christianity*, 109 –11.

Whispering,
"Surely you will not know death!
Instead,
You will have greater knowledge,
Little gods would weep to know
as much as you."

Such knowledge kills,
For it is written you will weep.
Weep for yourselves,
Weep dragon tears,
For you who bite are bitten,
Stained by lies
that scar the soul,
and bury deep.

Are you listening to a dragon?
Don't believe a thing he says.
Dragons lie.

I heard one calling at the altar,
"Set your careless offering before the LORD.
He does not mind.
One sheaf of wheat is like another."

But the listener's brother
lives a better way.
Man,
Beware.
You have become the dragon,
Crouching at the door,
Desiring blood.
Your anger sours,
Covets,
Murders love to savor pride.

Too late.
The dragon's lies have given birth,
And mercy died.

Are you listening to a dragon?
Don't believe a thing he says.
Dragons lie.

I heard one sighing,
"I have wisdom for this hour.
Hope is cowered,
Patience dying.
Without a prophet,
Only omens, sorceries, and entrails
teach our actions."
Who could reach beyond the silence
but a dragon?

Only death
could call the dead.
Only dark and misery
unwind the future.
Did you hear that dragons lie?
One who sits here has forgotten.
Now he hangs,
Without his head.

Are you listening to a dragon?
Don't believe a thing he says.
Dragons lie.

They felt it tickling their ear,
A passing thought, like smoke.
Who wouldn't want
their names be lifted high,
Their standing
far above the shoulders of the common crowd?
Be seen as righteous
in the eyes of the apostles?
Devoted largesse
paints a status rising up before the saints.
What else is money for?

But not too much,
Don't give it all away.

For dragon hearts
have trouble with their loot.
Such money lovers keep a tighter hold,
And make all men and women liars
when they claim to give away the wealth they own.

Devoted cannot be renamed.
And Ananias and Sapphira find
their souls instead
have been reclaimed.
Who wouldn't want
their names be lifted high,
Their standing
far above the shoulders of the common crowd?
As so they are.
Remembered as two lives exchanged
For what they are,
For what they own.
They are the dead.

Are you listening to a dragon?
Don't believe a thing he says.
Dragons lie.

In The Trenches

Look up Genesis 3:1–7; Genesis 4:3–8; I Samuel 28:3–19; Acts 5:1–11.

1. What are the dangers of listening to dragons?

2. What kinds of temptations do dragons use?

Day 4

Scouting the Territory

Welcome to the collegiate world of the Royal Me; the need to elevate self and all its myriad feelings to personal godhead above all else, to become the perfect victim. "I am offended," could be the dragon motto. Ordinary and indifferent questions, comments, and actions long thought innocent are now heavily weighted; intrusive and intentionally destructive. Toni Airaksinen, News Correspondent at Campus Reform, an on-line college news source, writes that Smith College has hired an outside company to run a 24/7 hotline for students feeling plagued with unwanted and unwelcome offenses; including not only spoken words, but graffiti, written messages, or images.[3]

This is not just a terrible shame, but a grotesque mangling and deconstruction of language and common life. The fruits of the Tower of Babel—disengagement—have reached new lows. Now confusion and distrust between different languages has become intentional enmity between speakers of the same words. No more universally accepted boundaries that allow for differences and create opportunities to foster diversity, or build cultural growth, consensus, and companionship. Just free floating, ever-changing personal moments of hurts with double meanings—irrational slights that conceive dragon-sized self aggrandizations. The truly sad irony of all this is that the same people who see offense lurking around every question and comment, every picture or advertisement, are starving for solidarity, a connection, a community they can call their own. We were created as social beings, and that desire never leaves us. We want to find a place where everybody knows our name, where we are understood.

Instead, total self-absorption has given birth to total disconnection. Dragons laugh. Division is Satan's victory. Misunderstandings are his joy. Words, simple words, turned into missiles of accusation are his deepest pleasure. It seems a terrible shame to feed dragons. But the Royal Me, only thinking of self, is blinded by self, and does not see the horror in front of it. "I am offended" now has all the blessings of the Destroyer. Words isolate. Speech is dangerous. Even pictures are disguised attacks. Hell has begun in earnest.

---

3. Airaksinen, "Smith College hires firm."

While dragons praise division, God has always been about reconciliation. Sometimes we forget that outside of Christ, we are already enemies with each other in search of a war. We may talk big about peace, but since Genesis 3, we have been at war with God and with each other. Adam and Eve no longer trust each other and look for blame; Cain kills Abel. We have been looking at this all wrong. Finding offense is easy. Overlooking offense or offering forgiveness is what is truly hard. And our forgiveness is tainted. We either clap ourselves on the back for being so charitable to the undeserving, or just as secretly keep that grudge. He didn't deserve it. I just said he did. And how quick are we to overlook an undeserved offense toward us?

Romans 5 tells us that Christians are people that were loved and forgiven by God while we were enemies (Rom 5:10), recognizing that only the blood of Christ saved us from ourselves, and the continual working of the Holy Spirit is what compels us to become agents of reconciliation, even as Christ himself reconciled, and continues to reconcile us. C.S. Lewis put it succinctly: "To be a Christian means to forgive the inexcusable, because God has forgiven the inexcusable in you."[4]

How can we be reconcilers? God's world overflows with words. Christ is called the Word in John 1. He is the "Word made flesh" dwelling with us. Hebrews describes Christ as the "radiance of the glory of God and the exact imprint of his nature," and that "he upholds the universe by the word of his power" (Heb 1:3). God created the universe with words. Jesus calmed the storm with words. He said, "It is finished" (John 19:30), and the work of redemption was accomplished. Divine words are actions with cosmic and eternal consequences. If we belong to Christ, we are word people, too. As fellow citizen with the saints, and members of the household of God (the place where we are truly known by our names), we have been given the task to sanctify words, to temper words with grace, to offer words of truth, honor, and praise. We must be aware that our tongue has the potential to be a fire, a restless evil. We are called to repent, and instead of offend, sow seeds of peace (Jas 3:13–18). Our words have consequences as well.

Our job is three-fold. First, speak the truth. The gospel is already an offense to those who do not believe, (1 Pet 2:8) and we must never trade security for truth. Second, we must speak in love. Be sensitive to the weaker among us who only see words as personal attacks. And finally, be ready to accept this world's unfair attacks for the sake of Christ. For out of words of

4. Lewis, *Weight of Glory,* 182.

grace and a heart of forgiveness come the community that the world still longs for, and the opportunity for discourse and peace. Out of words of divine reconciliation can come the very whiff of heaven.

In The Trenches

1. Our God is a God of words. How does The Dragon use words to destroy us?

2. How can we use speech and actions to mend, to bring peace, to bring hope?

Day 5

Heart Check

1. Read James 1:19–20.

2. Can you think of a time when not speaking at all might bring peace?

3. When speaking might bring hope and encouragement?

Week 21—Fan Wars

Day 1

Studying the Battle Plan

"Put on then, as God's chosen ones, holy and beloved, compassionate hearts, kindness, humility, meekness, and patience, bearing with one another and, if one has a complaint against another, forgiving each other; as the Lord has forgiven you, so you also must forgive . . . And let the peace of Christ rule in your hearts, to which indeed you were called in one body. And be thankful. Let the word of Christ dwell in you richly, teaching and admonishing one another in all wisdom, singing psalms and hymns and spiritual songs, with thankfulness in your hearts to God. And whatever you do, in word or deed, do everything in the name of the Lord Jesus, giving thanks to God the Father through him" (Col 3:12–13, 15–17).

In The Trenches

1. What does it mean to "bear with one another?"
2. How can being thankful change a difficult situation?

Day 2

Scouting the Territory

The summers in Maryland are known to be hot and humid, even late into the evening. Eighty degrees may be cooler than ninety degrees by the thermometer reading, but when you are lying on sticky, warm sheets, and the air is filled with moisture, nothing feels comfortable or cool. We didn't have air conditioning when I was growing up, so every summer night was a ritual of cool baths and fans.

We lived in a two–story colonial with a whole house fan on the second floor. Its purpose was to draw the hot air accumulated in the house during the day to bypass the upstairs, and be blown out through the attic vents above. As long as the air was moving, our rooms were bearable, and sleep was possible.

Our family, like all families, was made up of a community of very different people. We may have shared interests and a general vision for life, but we didn't think or act the same. That should have made us more interesting and complementary, as we had different strengths and weaknesses. But our sinful nature and self–centeredness always seemed to get in the way. One of my sisters was very sensitive to sound, particularly at night. I remember she wrapped a family alarm clock in at least two knitted winter hats to muffle its constant ticking. She may have liked the feel of cool air. But to her, sound was the enemy of sleep, and the loud hum of the fan her nemesis.

Just when we were all drifting off to sleep at last, this sensitive soul would get up and turn off the fan. Without the flow of air, we were once again adrift in an oven. Soon another sister would get up and turn the machine back on. Ah. Breeze again. But only for a moment, as sister number one went back to turn it off. The Fan Wars had begun. On. Off. On. Off. Cool. Hot. Cool. Hot. Pretty soon the two siblings would be standing under the switch, slapping each other's hands away in an effort to become Queen of the Fan.

Finally my father would get up in a huff, growl appropriately at both offenders, and set the fan at "medium"—too loud for one, and not cool enough for the rest of us. Compromise. And so it went all summer long. We all laugh about it now, but I have to wonder—why didn't anyone think to get that poor child some earplugs?

And so it is with families—different people with different needs trying to find acceptable compromises, and generally being irritated, frustrated, and occasionally combative in the attempt. The church is a family as well, with a shared vision for Christ and his gospel. That vision is our goal—to serve Christ in worship and obedience, and then proclaim the good news of salvation to ourselves and our neighbor. "But you are a chosen race, a royal priesthood, a holy nation, a people for his own possession, that you may proclaim the excellencies of him who called you out of darkness into his marvelous light" (1 Pet 2:9).

There is our purpose. Now how do we get along? We are not clones, and sometimes we get in each other's way instead of walking side by side. This problem of getting in each other's way, even when we are headed in the right direction for the right cause, is universal. At the church in Philippi, apparently two women were having trouble getting along. "I entreat Euodia and I entreat Syntyche," writes Paul, "to agree in the Lord. Yes, I ask you also true companion, help these women, who have labored side by side with me in the gospel together with Clement and the rest of my fellow workers, whose names are in the book of life" (Phil 4:2–3). Work it out, ladies. And to the rest of the congregation: help them. Recognize that disagreements are meant to make us kinder and more compassionate toward each other, not slapping each other's hands away. They are opportunities to help us overcome our weaknesses, and draw together in stronger bonds of unity and love.

"Beloved," writes John, "If God so loved us, we also ought to love one another" (1 John 4:11). Paul is even more specific: "Do nothing from rivalry or conceit, but in humility count others more significant than yourselves" (Phil 2:3). And then he tells us what that looks like. Christ didn't exploit his advantages as God when it came to us. He became low, a servant for our sake, and loved us all the way to the cross. Because of what Jesus accomplished, we are enabled through the Holy Spirit to bear with each other's weaknesses and forgive each other, even as God in Christ forgave us. You who have been reconciled with Christ, reach out and reconcile with each other.

The Fan Wars taught me about differences, about loving someone who could be irritating, about seeing the world through other eyes (and sensitive ears). It taught me about being family even when it was difficult, about accepting discomfort for the sake of the other. "Keep loving one another earnestly," adds Peter, "since love covers a multitude of sins" (1 Pet 4:8).

Love does cover a multitude of sins, whether it is in our individual families, or the larger community of saints that define our particular church. And God uses both the sinful and delightful quirks in each of us—in our family, our friends, and our neighbors, to teach us how to develop compassionate hearts, kindness, humility, meekness and patience (Col 3:12). It can be a painful thing. I for one am still learning how to love. But I am also learning about having a sense of humor about the whole lifelong adventure!

In The Trenches

1. What does love look like in actions and words?

2. Worship of and obedience to Christ means loving actions come first. *Feeling* loving comes second. How does Christ help us accomplish this?

Day 3

Postings from the Front

"There are times when we put our trust in a person (something created) and what we can get from that person *rather than* putting our trust in Christ and loving others. Once again, it comes down to spiritual allegiances. Like the ancient idolaters, we have said that God is not enough . . . The feeling of emptiness is usually a sign that we have put our trust in something that can't sustain us . . . We were created to enjoy the many things God gives without making them the center of our lives. When we confuse the two, our lives feel out of kilter. To feel better, we try again and search for love apart from God, but when we finally realize that it is elusive, we forsake the quest and quietly despair . . . Life is ultimately about God . . . When you get to God, don't stop until he surprises you with his beauty and love, which shouldn't take too long. After all, if you can find mixed allegiances, dual allegiances, spiritual unfaithfulness, or a wandering heart in your life, you are essentially guilty of spiritual adultery, and, contrary to your expectations, your God delights in your return."—Edward T. Welch[1]

1. Welch, *Depression*, 114–15.

1. Where does love come from?

2. How does Dr. Welch say that worshiping idols interferes with loving others?

Day 4

In The Trenches

1. Read Psalm 36:5; Isaiah 54:10; Lamentations 3:22–24; and 1 John 4:7–21.

2. How big is God's love for you?

3. How does God's love for us free us to love one another?

Day 5

Heart Check

"Now to him who is able to do far more abundantly than all that we ask or think, according to the power at work within us, to him be glory in the church and in Christ Jesus throughout all generations, forever and ever. Amen. I therefore, a prisoner for the Lord, urge you to walk in a manner worthy of the calling to which you have been called, with all humility and gentleness, with patience, bearing with one another in love, eager to maintain the unity of the Spirit in the bond of peace" (Eph 3:20–4:3).

1. What am I called to do?

2. How can I possibly do what I am called to do?

3. Do you sense Paul's reassurance and confidence in these verses?

Week 22—Faith that Frees

Day 1

Studying the Battle Plan

"On that day, when evening had come, he [Jesus] said to them, 'Let us go across to the other side.' And leaving the crowd, they took him with them in the boat, just as he was. And other boats were with him. And a great windstorm arose, and the waves were breaking into the boat, so that the boat was already filling. But he was in the stern, asleep on the cushion. And they woke him and said to him, 'Teacher, do you not care that we are perishing?' And he awoke and rebuked the wind and said to the sea, 'Peace! Be still!' And the wind ceased, and there was a great calm. He said to them, 'Why are you so afraid? Have you still no faith?' And they were filled with great fear and said to one another, 'Who then is this, that even the wind and the sea obey him?'" (Mark 4:35–41)

In The Trenches

1. What does this episode in the life of Jesus tell us about him?

2. Did the disciples really understand who Jesus was? Why or why not?

Day 2

Scouting the Territory

The frightening daily news and depressing articles on social media paint pictures of a world gone mad. I am fighting a battle with fear again. Like taunting whispers of dragon smoke in my ears, fear fights to annihilate my faith, and it is a daily battle. But faith looks above the battle and "sees" the Warrior King. Faith is not hoping and wishing it will come out okay. Faith is focused on the Warrior King; his love, his sacrifice, and his power over death and sin. Faith sees victory before it happens because the Warrior King has already been and will forever be victorious. He created with his word, he rules by his word, and he will win with his word. I am his by his word, and as I read his word, I have seen the power of his word. But some days I am still blind and afraid because I am listening to the dragons.

Luke 7:1–10 describes a man who was a model of faith. He was a Gentile, a Roman centurion, who sought Jesus to heal his beloved servant. We know from Luke's account that this commander loved the Jewish people and arranged the building of the local synagogue in Capernaum. He is a man accustomed to authority who doesn't presume he can speak directly to Jesus, but sends his request through respected Jewish elders. He also knows that Jesus has the kind of authority that can overcome disease with only a word. He sends messengers ahead, and asks Jesus to just say the words of healing. well aware of the barriers between Jews and Gentiles. But his faith overcomes those barriers because his faith is in the Creator, the One who heals with a word, who breathes life where there is none.

The disciples, meanwhile, are living among God's miracles. They see them every day. Everywhere they go with Jesus, the dead rise, the lame walk, the blind see, and sins are forgiven. But these men might as well be dead, lame, and blind because they do not yet believe. They do not yet truly know who Jesus is. In the infancy of their faith, they are God's contrast to the centurion. They haven't quite grasped that they are walking daily in the presence of God himself, the Creator. Surely the one who heals, and at the same time forgives sin can only be the Creator! They see it. They know it, yet they do not yet really understand it. It will take the resurrection from the dead after the horrors of the crucifixion, the meetings in the locked upper room, and the meal of fish beside the lake to truly open their eyes. But they are learning.

At one of their great moments of fear, Jesus is the one who stills raging wind and water with a word. He rebukes the wind and storm into silence and they are suddenly afraid. They begin to understand if only for this moment, with whom they are dealing. It is a moment of frightening clarity. "Why were you afraid of the storm?" Jesus asks them; his unspoken thought hangs in the air— Why are you afraid of the storm when the wind and the waves must obey me?

It must have given them pause, as Scripture records their heart–stopping fear. It should give us a respectful, sober pause as well. This is not the fear of the storm, or the fear of disease, but the fear of the Lord, and here is where faith begins. It is all about knowing who our God is, and what he has done for us. Our faith is intended to be focused on Jesus. We are to "look to Jesus, the founder and perfecter of our faith," (Heb 12:2) because Jesus is the reality and substance of all of our hope. We are his joy, says the writer of Hebrews, and for us Christ endured the cross, despising the shame, and is now seated at the right hand of the throne of God. He swallowed our death and will someday destroy that great dragon, Satan, and all of death forever. With dragons on the prowl, there is much to fear, and we who walk in God's company are not immune from fears and worries. But our faith is not intended to be blind. It is faith that "sees" into eternity, where Christ intercedes for us. It is faith that fears God and not the battle. Take your eyes off the trials, the dangers, the dragons. "Just one word," should be your prayer. "Just speak the word, Lord. I know you will carry me through."

In The Trenches

1. What or whom is the focus of true faith?
2. Where does true faith begin?

Day 3

Studying the Battle Plan

"Though the fig tree should not blossom, nor fruit be on the vines, the produce of the olive fail and the fields yield no food, the flock be cut off from the fold and there be no herd in the stalls, yet I will rejoice in the LORD; I will take joy in the God of my salvation.

GOD, the Lord, is my strength; he makes my feet like the deer's; he makes me tread on my high places" (Hab 3:17–19).

In The Trenches

1. Our joy cannot come from our circumstances. Our lives are too much of an uneven and unpredictable mixture of good and bad experiences. Who is our joy?

2. Why is he our joy?

Day 4

Dance with the River

Does He not stand in the River before me?
Someday I'll reach the other shore.
Where can I go but into the River?
Even floods fall at His command.

So I obey,
Still afraid of the waters,
I walk to the River,
My foot in the River,
A wild and thundering, frightening dance.
I see Him before me,
Standing before me,
Holding the waters away by His hand.

Where can I go but into the River?
He keeps me dry from the waters above,
I walk on by the waters below.
My foot will only touch the sand.
My dance with the River is leading me forward,
Is taking me closer to Promised Land.

In The Trenches

1. Read Joshua 3:9–17. How did the Israelites know they would walk through the river on dry land? Do you think it was hard to step into the river?

2. The river can be a metaphor for anything that is difficult or scary for you and me. How do we get across our "rivers"?

Day 5

Heart Check

1. Read Philippians 4:11–13.

2. What is the secret of joy in all circumstances? What is necessary for us to learn contentment?

Week 23—God's Lawnmower

Day 1

Studying the Battle Plan

"Now to him who is able to do far more abundantly than all that we ask or think according to the power at work within us, to him be glory in the church and in Christ Jesus throughout all generations, forever and ever. Amen" (Eph 3:20).

"And my God will supply every need of yours according to his riches in glory in Christ Jesus" (Phil 4:19).

In The Trenches

1. Do you believe God has the ability to take care of *all* your needs?

2. Have you experienced God's loving and special care?

Day 2

Scouting the Territory

We bought our first home many years ago on the Eastern Shore of Maryland. It was a tiny one–story rancher, in a small, picturesque town. It was new construction on an undeveloped lot—grass in the back, dirt in the front. We needed family help and a life insurance policy to make the down payment. So there was no extra money for a front lawn, sidewalk, or paved driveway. We managed to scrape enough together for a gravel driveway, and stepping stones to the front door to keep us out of the mud. But who had money for a lawnmower?

A friend from church offered his beat up old mower. "It hasn't worked for years, but it might work if you tinker with it a bit. You can have it for free." So we brought it home. Larry, my husband, decided to give it a try on a Saturday morning. He poured in some gas, and pumped. The mower grunted, growled, and rumbled to life. It worked! Soon the back yard was trimmed, and the mower was stored in a sheltered spot. For five years that rumpled, rusty mower did its job without complaint. I thought he said it didn't work? It worked fine for us.

Then my husband's job changed and it was time to move on. Our financial situation had improved as well. The new house was larger, and in a more upscale neighborhood. And we could finally afford a new lawnmower. The day we brought it home, the old, faithful mower stopped working. We thought we had probably gotten its best, last years of service.

A large family joined our church. With limited means, they were looking for help in settling into the area. We had some carpet to donate, as well as odds and ends of furniture. "You know," added my husband in passing, "we have this old lawnmower in the shed. It hasn't worked since we moved here, but you could have it if you want." It was an afterthought on our part, and it got it out of the shed. The man smiled. "I enjoy fixing things. Sure, we'll take it. You never know."

A few weeks later he called. "I don't know why you said the mower doesn't work. Works fine. Didn't need to fix a thing. Thank you so much for your generosity. The place is starting to feel like home at last." We hung up the phone and looked at each other. Our castoffs were treasures to someone else. And we had been the guardians of a true treasure we hadn't fully appreciated— God's lawnmower; the mower that only worked for those in need of it. The mower that signified his grace. Carpet and furniture are only things. Bigger and better houses are only things. But a mower that worked only when needed—"And my God will supply every need of yours according to his riches in glory in Christ Jesus" (Phil 4:19)—that was truly a priceless gift!

"I have learned in whatever situation I am to be content," writes Paul in Philippians 4. "I know how to be brought low and I know how to abound. In any and every circumstance, I have learned the secret of facing plenty and hunger, abundance and need. I can do all things through him who strengthens me" (Phil 4:11–13).

I may have more things now, but what I really require is Christ. I have experienced abundance and need, but what I really need is to be humbly trusting in his care no matter what the situation, because that is where I find him. I find contentment, and I find peace. I think I need more of God's lawnmowers in my life!

In The Trenches

1. A lawnmower is an ordinary object. How should knowing that God cares about working lawnmowers affect our daily trust in his provision?

2. Are you thankful for all of God's ordinary, everyday care?

Day 3

In The Trenches

1. Read Psalm 103. What a great God! There are so many things we can be thankful for. Make a list of all of God's blessings to his people named in this psalm.

2. Read Colossians 3:12–17. How can we express a thankful heart?

Day 4

Cracked Open

I used to see in only grey.
I didn't mind.
When grey is all there is,
It seems a comfort,
Stable,
Settling like an endless cloud
of personal security,
Where I design

The shades and shadows,
Silently dismissing
any sparks or flashes
on the edges of my space.
I called it grace.

It wasn't.
It was just grey.

Then He burst in
To grey,
To plain,
With brilliance,
God intruding
on an empty heart,
Breaking in
With overwhelming,
All amazing,
Blazing colors,
Lighting up my world
To see the blues of endless skies
And meadowed greens,
The reds of fire flowers,
Oranges and yellows shimmering
on tangerines,
A rainbow panoply
of glorious intensity.

Not so stable,
Not so comfortable
or safe,
But oh, so real.

Brighter.
Sharper.
More alive,
More tender,
And more jarring,

Wildly cluttering my strife,
Unbounding,
Filling me with life
and wonder.
Now I see,
I truly see
When He
stepped in
and broke through me.

In The Trenches

What happens when we practice a lifestyle of thankfulness?

Day 5

Heart Check

"His [Job's] wife said to him, 'Are you still maintaining your integrity? Curse God and die!' He replied, 'You are talking like a foolish woman. Shall we accept good from God, and not trouble?' In all this, Job did not sin in what he said" (Job 2:9–10 NIV).

When I think of the opposite of thankfulness, I think of complaining, discontent, and sometimes bitterness. All these responses show a disdain for God, the author and giver of all things. A discontent heart is not a worshipping heart. How can thanksgiving lead us back toward worship and a contented spirit?

Foot Soldiers

"Wait for the LORD; be strong, and let your heart take courage; wait for the LORD" (Ps 27:14).

Week 24—Iron Sharpens Iron

Day 1

Studying the Battle Plan

"But we have this treasure in jars of clay, to show that the surpassing power belongs to God and not to us. We are afflicted in every way, but not crushed; perplexed, but not driven to despair; persecuted, but not forsaken; struck down, but not destroyed; always carrying in the body the death of Jesus, so that the life of Jesus may also be manifested in our bodies. For we who live are always being given over to death for Jesus' sake, so that the life of Jesus also may be manifested in our mortal flesh. So death is at work in us, but life in you" (2 Cor 4:7–12).

In The Trenches

1. What does God say about the purpose of human weaknesses?
2. How then should we view our own suffering and weaknesses?

Day 2

Studying the Battle Plan

"Preserve me, O God, for in you I take refuge.
I say to the LORD, 'You are my Lord;
I have no good apart from you.'

As for the saints in the land, they are the excellent ones,
in whom is all my delight.
The sorrows of those who run after another god shall multiply;
their drink offerings of blood I will not pour out
or take their names on my lips.

The LORD is my chosen portion and my cup;
you hold my lot.
The lines have fallen for me in pleasant places,
indeed, I have a beautiful inheritance.

I bless the LORD who gives me counsel;
in the night also my heart instructs me.
I have set the LORD always before me;
because he is at my right hand, I shall not be shaken.

Therefore my heart is glad, and my whole being rejoices;
my flesh also dwells secure.
For you will not abandon my soul to Sheol,
or let your holy one see corruption.

You make known to me the path of life;
in your presence there is fullness of joy;
at your right hand are pleasures forevermore" (Ps 16).

In The Trenches

1. List the promises God has made to us in Psalm 16. Which promises spoke to you?

2. What is the psalmist's attitude toward God?

Day 3

Scouting the Territory

Christ, the sacraments, and the preaching of the word are the lifeblood of the church. But I would propose to you that the widows, the singles, all who are lonely or feel invisible, and those who are experiencing great suffering, are the heart and soul of our churches. We need to hear the word preached, read it, and study it. But we also need to see it lived before us, particularly in the trenches. These people who suffer have been called by God (for reasons only he knows and understands) to walk through the fire before the rest of us. "Iron sharpens iron," writes the sage of Proverbs, "and one man sharpens another" (Prov 27:17). The picture is of an iron sword being sharpened by a whetting iron. It is a metaphor of true friendship where the one who loves is not afraid to speak a hard truth, even if it hurts, for the betterment of the person being criticized.[1] "Faithful are the wounds of a friend," says the writer in the same chapter (vs 6). In this case, the wounds are wounded people, and their hard truth to the rest of us is that God is stronger than death. They teach us that there is a walk of joy in an intensity that can only be experienced when one is totally dependent on him every hour of every day, through struggles with pain, loss, and death. I have seen it lived in front of me.

We glibly sing that we are the family of God. We say we will pray for someone, and then walk away past another invisible person; dropping a cheery smile before our cup of fellowship coffee. Connections missed, we move on to the next person. If this is us, we have not yet been wounded enough. The wound that encourages, the wound that matures us and draws us nearer to Christ, is the wound that takes us out of safe places and puts us in the world of the invisible sufferer. It is when we visit them in the hospital and pray for them, when we begin to notice whether they made it to church or not, when we send an email or card that we really get to know them as people, that their wounds bear beautiful fruit in us. This is when we begin to finally understand how the gospel is meant to be lived out. "Faith by itself," writes James, if it does not have works, "is dead" (Jas 2:17). If we truly are alive in Christ, we should be exhibiting his love, his compassion. No one should be invisible in the family of God.

Sometimes we must become the wounded to appreciate how much love is intended to be shared with the body of Christ and with those outside of Christ. I watched God do this with my sister Sheila. I talk about my sister Sheila often because God used her to teach me so much. I remember taking her to a cancer center in Boston for her next chemo treatment. I could feel her discomfort, her edginess, as we signed her in for treatment. The room was very large, filled with other uncomfortable women perched on dull brown padded chairs that lined the walls of the space, creating a silent circle

1. Waltke, Proverbs, 384

of withdrawn, eyes–down creatures, attached to slowly dripping IV tubes. Everything about the place was antiseptic, barren, and cold. They all had knitted hats on to cover bald heads. The silence was palpable and painful.

Once Sheila was settled in and her IV inserted, she relaxed into her chair, whipped off her hat to display her delightfully bald head, and turned her attention to the ladies in the room. "Beth!" she called across the room. Beth looked up, surprised. "How did your son do at his recital?" Beth smiled, relating a happy experience. They talked for a while, and slowly Beth relaxed, removed her fuzzy cap. "Carol," said Sheila, moving to the next woman in the circle. "Did your husband have a good meeting with the client?" And Carol was off and running with her story. And so it went, one woman at a time, being remembered and cared for. Soon all the hats were off and cheerful chatter filled the room. The place seemed brighter, lighter, and warmer than it had been before. It was. Because the love of Christ was being shed abroad by one who understood their suffering and was willing to enter in. Many of these women died before Sheila did, but they died in the Lord because of her love for them.

Those who suffer have much to tell us, much to share about the grace and love of Christ if we would only walk a little way with them into their world. They are given to us to pray for, to teach us how to live the gospel with compassion, how to truly love. They are meant to be the wounds of a friend. Iron does sharpen iron. For the sake of Christ, let the invisible in your church wound you.

In The Trenches

1. What can we learn from those who suffer?

2. How can we enter into their suffering in ways that encourage, comfort and uplift them?

Day 4

Pneuma

Pneuma.
Breath.
We could be skin,

Muscle,
Sinew stretching
bone to bone.

We could be odd machines alone,
Materials invented
out of man's desiring to be king,
Imagination
strutting in the wilderness.

We are attracted,
Mesmerized by manners,
Wealth and status,
All the sensibilities
that make
A man,
A woman,
Shine above the crowd.

We think we've plumbed
the depths
of life's philosophies,
When we behold ourselves.
Remarking,
With that element of condescending taste,
Refined
Sophisticated,
Smug,
Distrusting any absolutes
(Except our own),
"How grand the search,
The everlasting search,"
Expressions delving far beyond infinitude,
Our brilliance
Giving meaning to our monuments
of vapid stone.
Yet there's the shroud.

Deus Ex Machina.
The breath of God resounds.
We are not gods,
We are His miracles,
His vast creation, not our own.

We act as if the stage is ours
to bend,
Manipulate at will,
Our stories to be told.
We recreate.
We kill.
We die.
"Breathe on these slain,"
We cry,
"That they may live!"

And so He breathes.
And ever after New Creation
rises from the dirt,
Like dry bones in the wilderness,
Bone to bone
To sinew,
Wrapped in skin,
The heart of His imagination
breathes in us,
For glorious Grace and Life has entered in.

In The Trenches

1. Pneuma means "breath." Genesis 2:7 explains the creation of man. What made Adam human?

2. What makes us less human? What does the speaker in the poem desire from God?

Day 5

Heart Check

"Therefore, since we have been justified by faith, we have peace with God through our Lord Jesus Christ. Through him we have also obtained access by faith into this grace in which we stand, and we rejoice in hope of the glory of God. More than that, we rejoice in our sufferings, knowing that suffering produces endurance, and endurance produces character, and character produces hope, and hope does not put us to shame, because God's love has been poured into our hearts through the Holy Spirit who has been given to us" (Rom 5:1–5).

I want hope as I struggle in this hopeless world. I assume you do, too. How does this passage tell us we get there? Should the process require less dependence or more dependence on God?

Week 25—Battle Scars

Day 1

Studying the Battle Plan

"Behold, now is the favorable time; behold, now is the day of salvation. We put no obstacle in anyone's way, so that no fault may be found with our ministry, but as servants of God we commend ourselves in every way: by great endurance, in afflictions, hardships, calamities, beatings, imprisonments, riots, labors, sleepless nights, hunger; by purity, knowledge, patience, kindness, the Holy Spirit, genuine love; by truthful speech, and the power of God; with the weapons of righteousness for the right hand and for the left; through honor and dishonor, through slander and praise. We are treated as impostors, and yet are true; as unknown and yet well known; as dying, and behold, we live; as punished, and yet not killed; as sorrowful, yet always rejoicing; as poor, yet making many rich; as having nothing, yet possessing everything" (2 Cor 6:2b–10).

In The Trenches

1. In this new section we talk about being a foot soldier in our war against The Dragon. None of us experience life exactly the same way, but what can it be like to be a foot soldier for Christ?

2. What weapons does God, through the Holy Spirit, give us to fight dragons without and dragons within?

Day 2

Scouting the Territory

Being a foot soldier in God's army can feel like a daunting task. We are not an elite fighting force. We are wounded and worn out, carrying all sorts of baggage: addiction, shame, selfishness, and pride. We struggle with our relationships. We have failing bodies, anxieties, and depression. We look put together on Sunday morning, but behind the suits, the outfits, and the new shoes, we are limping. We are vulnerable, suffering, worried, and confused citizens of heaven trying to manage on earth. We are ordinary people wrestling with the weaknesses in ourselves and our world. We are an army with battle scars.

But here is the amazing truth of the gospel. God the Father chose us. He didn't need us. He is complete in himself. He chose to love us, and bring us into relationship with him. Jesus the Son made that relationship possible. He died for us. He took all our rebellion and our suffering on himself. And then he offered his perfect life for us before the Father, so that when God sees us, he sees Christ's perfection. In his resurrection he conquered death for us. And he turned to us and said, "Now I choose you to be the heirs of all that I have. It's yours, and my Comforter, the Holy Spirit will guide you in all truth." We who are the scarred, the lonely, the anxious, are also now the heirs of all that is beautiful. We have been gathered into an eternal communion of loving fellowship, and have been offered immense, soul–resting peace. We may be weak and limited in this life, but by eternity standards, we have been given everything. "I want you to start walking, start living for me—just the way you are, battle scars and all. I have work for you to do. Trust me."

So here we are—God's wounded army standing in the battlefield. We see our weakness. God sees Christ and his strength. He sees the Holy Spirit working within us. We have been commanded to put the weight of our lives on Christ, to let him carry our load. He knows we would be tempted to start depending on ourselves, so he keeps us a little off–balance, and a lot dependent on him. He leaves us with our battle scars intact. "My grace is sufficient for you," he says, "for my power is made perfect in weakness" (2 Cor 12:9). And off he sends us back to the war. We have been asked to keep our scars to show the power of Christ in the midst of suffering. We march forward proclaiming the life of Jesus by our obedience, and with our battle scars.

By his love and the working of the Holy Spirit, we can have cancer and make beauty and light out of the darkness. We may get old, forgetful, and full of pain, and yet bring joy and wisdom to friends and family. We struggle through depression or anxiety, and touch the lonely with Christ's love. The amazing truth is that we speak Christ and his resurrection power the loudest in our failures and weakness. We may be weary and shaky lights, shining quietly among those who are still stumbling around in the dark, but we are also his humble ministers of true peace and love. We are not just foot soldiers. We are the loved, the accepted, and we have been called to be walking, breathing pictures to the world of the immeasurable riches of his grace.

In The Trenches

1. Why does God leave us with our battle scars intact?

2. Are you a weary foot soldier? Read 2 Corinthians 6:2b–10 again. Do these verses bring you encouragement?

Day 3

Service

We come in our own weakness,
Serving each the other,
Reaching out
To love a friend,
To offer prayers.

We are the sick,
The lonely,
Impatiently aware of struggling cares,
So, so tired,
Some of us in pain.

But He Who Reigns Above,
Who became us,
Who was The Man as well as God,

He understands our drifting minds,
Our tethered hopes,
Our disappointments,
All our endless limitations,
Finiteness a freeze,
A liability,
A stumbling walk,
He gets it.

God With Us.
He lived with us.
He died for us.
And then He broke our stumbling free.
He lives.
We breathe.
At last.

We come in our own weakness,
Serving each the other,
Reaching out
To love a friend,
To offer prayers.
And suddenly the passing breeze
is filled with Life,
With hope,
With grace,
With possibilities.

We still are sick,
Still lonely,
Still impatiently aware of struggling cares,
Still tired,
Some of us in pain.

But now we do it all for Him,
Because of Him,
For His own sake,
We serve.

We dedicate our pain,
Our trials.
All we are
as arms of gratitude for His delight.
And as our eyes and hearts lean forward toward His face,
We gain.

In The Trenches

1. Here is a poetic picture of what we are talking about this week. In the context of this poem, what does God with us mean?

2. How do we find hope and grace in the midst of our trials?

Day 4

Love Song

Love skips instead of walking
when we're both too old to play.
Love listens to a tale
already told a thousand times.
It does not mind the quiet,
Not much time for shallow words.
It waits.
It breathes,
Caressing ancient hands
to trace old memories and worlds.

And the love goes on and on,
And it keeps on building,
Sowing more affection
than I could even know,
More lives Holy,
More lives loving,
Loving Him,
His love makes my loving grow.

Love doesn't hear the stammer,
Whether conversation flows.
Love sees the person
underneath the body's weaving dance.
It does not mind the noises,
Too much day to fill with hope.
It smiles,
It sings,
'Til laughter wreaths
Unfolding hearts afraid to be,
To cope.

And the love goes on and on,
And it keeps on building,
Sowing more affection
than I could even know,
More lives Holy,
More lives loving,
Loving Him,
His love makes my loving grow.

Love doesn't fear the dying
because Light has lit the path.
Love offered up a pardon
when I didn't have a chance.
He did not mind my quarrels
when He chose to set me free.
He died.
He paid my ransom,
Crushing Him,
But in His mercy
saving you and saving me.

And the love goes on and on,
And it keeps on building,
Sowing more affection
than I could even know,
More lives Holy,

More lives loving,

Loving Him,

His love makes my loving grow.

Postings from the Front

"The *new command* is simple enough for a toddler to memorize and appreciate, profound enough that the most mature believers are repeatedly embarrassed at how poorly they comprehend it and put it in to practice: *Love one another. As I have loved you, so you must love one another* . . . The more we recognize the depth of our own sin, the more we recognize the love of the Saviour; the more we appreciate the love of the Saviour, the higher his standard appears; the higher his standard appears, the more we recognize in our selfishness, our innate self–centeredness, the depth of our own sin. With a standard like this, no thoughtful believer can ever say, this side of the parousia, 'I am perfectly keeping the basic stipulation of the new covenant.'" —D.A. Carson.[1]

In The Trenches

1. How should knowing Christ loves you change the way you live?

2. How does loving one another change your attitudes about yourself and others?

3. Now read the poem, "Love Song." What makes your love grow?

Day 5

Heart Check

"For the love of Christ controls us, because we have concluded this: that one has died for all, therefore all have died; and he died for all, that those who live might no longer live for themselves but for him who for their sake died and was raised" (2 Cor 5:14–15).

How does Christ's love speak to the way you love others?

1. Carson, *Gospel According to John*, 484

Week 26—Trust and Obey

Day 1

Studying the Battle Plan

"The law of the LORD is perfect, reviving the soul; the testimony of the LORD is sure, making wise the simple; the precepts of the LORD are right, rejoicing the heart; the commandment of the LORD is pure, enlightening the eyes" (Ps 19:7–8).

"By this we know that we love the children of God, when we love God and obey his commandments. For this is the love of God, that we keep his commandments. And his commandments are not burdensome. For everyone who has been born of God overcomes the world. And this is the victory that has overcome the world— our faith. Who is it that overcomes the world except the one who believes that Jesus is the Son of God?" (1 John 5: 2–5)

In The Trenches

1. Notice all the names for Scripture. What are they? What kind of people do we become when we read and know Scripture?

2. Why is love so important in our understanding of obedience?

Day 2

Scouting the Territory

Trust and obey. Sometimes I think this is the hardest thing for a Christian to do. We prefer to plan our own lives, to make choices that are the most comfortable, and the least likely to cause inconvenience. Jesus said, "You shall love the Lord your God with all your heart and with all your soul and with all your mind. This is the great and first commandment" (Matt 22:37–38). Love me first, he says. "Abide in me. I am the vine, you are the branches . . . If you keep my commandments, you will abide in my love" (Jn. 15:4, 10). Get your priorities straight. I am in charge. Find out where I want you to go, and follow me. That's what he told his disciples— follow me. If you really love me, he says, you will obey me. And our obedience is a step by step, day by day, hour by hour, hanging tight to Jesus. We rest on his work on our behalf. And we trust he has put us right where he wants us, even when such obedience to him may involve being uncomfortable or uncertain, even when we think we have a "better way" than the one he has presently proscribed.

Being properly obedient requires a singular focus on the one we are trusting in. I am reminded of a pivotal scene in C.S. Lewis's, *The Silver Chair*. The children, Eustace Scrubb and Jill Pole, and their compatriot Puddleglum, an odd earthy and frog–like creature with a sober disposition, have been given a quest to find a lost prince. One of the signs Aslan gave them said that they would know the lost prince because he would ask them to do something in Aslan's name. The scene occurs at the point in the story where they are witnessing a raging dark knight, a man seemingly out of his wits, bound to an enchanted chair. They have been told not to unleash him, whatever he says because he is mortally dangerous. Their lives depend on remaining steadfast. They are expecting cunning lies in his request for freedom. What they don't expect is his anguished cry: "I adjure you to set me free. By all fears and all loves, by the bright skies of Overland, by the great Lion, by Aslan himself, I charge you."[1] It is a horrifying moment. The man has obviously fulfilled the sign, but they hesitate. The knight himself has told them that he is dangerous, that to obey him in this enchanted state is to court death. It is Puddleglum who clears the air. "Aslan didn't tell Pole what would happen. He only told her what to do. That fellow will be the death of

1. Lewis, *The Silver Chair*, 166.

us once he's up, I shouldn't wonder. But that doesn't let us off following the sign."[2] The point is, they are trusting and obeying Aslan first, not trusting what is happening around them. They have put their trust in a person, not their circumstances.

Our world, like Lewis's enchanted Underworld, is a false place full of misleading and untrustworthy people and situations. What looks attractive or merely logical and reasonable may be deadly. What looks difficult, takes us out of our comfort zones, and sometimes even threatens us, may be the safest place in the universe. We are only headed in the right direction when God sets the agenda and we follow. We can only choose correctly when we are trusting and obeying the right person. And that person is Jesus Christ, the one who stood between us and the wrath of God the Father, the one who still stands as our advocate before the very throne of heaven.

In The Trenches

1. Why does putting our trust in a person rather than our circumstance make such a difference?

2. When is it difficult to obey and to trust Christ?

Day 3

Postings from the Front

"These things I have spoken to you while I am still with you. But the Helper, the Holy Spirit, whom the Father will send in my name, he will teach you all things and bring to your remembrance all that I have said to you. Peace I leave with you; my peace I give to you. Not as the world gives do I give to you. Let not your heart be troubled, neither let it be afraid . . . Take heart. I have overcome the world" (John 14:25–27, 16:33).

"Everything changed when Jesus came. He died for sins, rose from the grave, and then, at Pentecost, sent the Spirit. The professional religious caste was no longer the titled few. Now followers of Jesus have all the competencies needed to encourage and instruct each other.

2. Lewis, *The Silver Chair*, 167

That is the reason we even consider helping others. We live in the age of the Spirit. Apart from Pentecost, we would be referral agents who simply introduce needy people to the real experts. We would hold our tongue for fear that we would just make matters worse. With the Spirit, we move toward other people and are amazed that God uses ordinary people to do his kingdom work."—Edward T. Welch.[3]

In The Trenches

1. Why can we have confidence in obeying Christ?

2. Is there anything that can separate us from God's love and sovereign care?

Day 4

God With Skin On

We might as well be death with legs,
No arms for reaching out,
Except to self.
My life,
My wants,
My endless needs
in strata,
Built up layer upon layer,
Like myopic oysters
in a maddening edifice of encrustation.
But there's no pearl.
Stone hearts weigh too much to carry pain.
Whom shall I send, and who will go for us?

Such black holes of indifference
are only echoes,
Vast repeating,
On and on reverberating,

3. Welch, *Side by Side*, 68.

Reaffirming my own name.

Keep on hearing,

Do not hear.

Keep on seeing,

Do not see.

I need something,

Someone

far beyond my vacant need.

How long, O Lord?

How long must I be dull,

Must I be lost,

Forsaken,

Empty?

Shriveled under judgment now displayed,

I am Forsaken,

Burned,

A useless stump.

Whom shall I send, and who will go for us?

The Holy Seed is in the stump,

The wood discarded,

Life rejected,

Life disdained,

Life gravely wounded

treads into my dark,

And takes my pain.

His heart is light.

His heart is life.

His heart is not afraid of troubled grief,

He knows full well.

For He who lived among us,

He the very Heart of Heaven,

All His glory layer upon layer,

Took our staggering weight,

Our vagrancy,

Our cosmic rootlessness,

Our death,

Our cross.
Beloved became Forsaken
for our gain.

And we are turned
From stone to flesh,
From shriveled egos into souls,
Whom shall I send and who will go for us?

He did.
How can I not respond
when all forsakenness is gone?
He gave me arms,
So I will hug.
He gave me legs,
So I will serve.
He fills my heart
to reach into another's life.
No policies,
No changes first before I touch a damaged heart.

Because He died,
My death is gone.
Because He lives,
My pain is light.
He carries me,
I carry, too.
That's Love at work,
That's ears to hear,
That's eyes to see,
That's Holy Life.
That's God with skin on.

In The Trenches

1. How am I able to express Christ and his love to others?
2. Describe what "God with skin on" means to you.

Day 5

Heart Check

This is the fourth verse from a favorite hymn, "Whate'er My God Ordains is Right."

> Whate'er my God ordains is right:
> here shall my stand be taken;
> though sorrow, need, or death be mine,
> yet am I not forsaken.
> My Father's care is round me there;
> he holds me that I cannot fall;
> and so to him I leave it all.[4]

What or who is our confidence in?

> "Will not the Judge of all the earth do right?" (Gen 18:25b NIV)

---

4. Rodigast, *Trinity Hymnal,* 108.

Week 27—Love in the Trenches

Day 1

Studying the Battle Plan

"For you formed my inward parts; you knitted me together in my mother's womb. I praise you, for I am fearfully and wonderfully made . . . Your eyes saw my unformed substance; in your book were written, every one of them, the days that were formed for me, when as yet there was none of them" (Ps 139:13–14, 16).

"For we are his workmanship, created in Christ Jesus for good works, which God prepared beforehand, that we should walk in them" (Eph 2:10).

In The Trenches

1. From conception to the day we die, we are in God's hands; every single moment. This truth will probably not take away the pain we experience, but it should give us tremendous hope, and the will to keep moving forward. What do these verses tell us about God's relationship to us, every step of the way?

2. How should such hope affect our attitudes and actions?

Day 2

Scouting the Territory

Finding out you are pregnant, when you wanted a child, is exhilarating. Finding out that the baby is already dying before it leaves the womb is crushing. And the pressure to terminate the pregnancy can be intense. Don't carry. Don't suffer. Start over. We keep trying to set out the rules of what makes life valuable. Is it quality? Is it the best choice for us? "In more recent times, newborn infants have been killed because family resources could not be stretched to accommodate another child, the child was disabled or ill, or the child was the 'wrong' gender."[1] Is it less suffering? Whatever you do, don't suffer. This is pain at its most intense, and we can appreciate the desire to end it as soon as possible; to find a way to wrap such agony into a box and walk away.

This world forgets that getting rid of the child doesn't end the suffering. It just complicates it. Not only is the baby gone, but the mother and father's souls are damaged. There was no joy in the child, no beauty in his life, however long or short, and no dignity in his death. Paul says that Jesus' followers have lives already destined for good works. Who is to say that this child's good work might be to declare the image and glory of God in his one day? Or that his parents' love and devotion displayed before a watching world might reveal the dignity and grace of his personhood?

My church understands this. When a young couple discovered they were expecting a terminally ill child, they were devastated. But the church of Jesus Christ is about seeing life and suffering through a different lens. The women of the church held a shower for this young couple. Who knew how long the baby would live? They celebrated his life. When he was born, the couple's relatives surrounded this young family. They prayed. They sang hymns. The boy only lived a few short hours, but his life and the lives of his family shed abroad the love of Christ among many who witnessed his birth, his life, and his death.

We cannot do this on our own without Christ's work for us, and the Holy Spirit's continuing work in us. For it is Christ's suffering that makes us whole, giving us the ability to "rejoice in our sufferings, knowing that suffering produces endurance, and endurance produces character, and character produces hope, and hope does not put us to shame, because God's

---

1. Ciampa, "Infanticide: Children as Chattel," 6.

love has been poured into our hearts through the Holy Spirit who has been given to us." (Rom. 5:3–5)

Suffering for the sake of Christ grows us; making us more compassionate and kind people. Our weakness, our suffering, makes us more able to notice and care for other weak people. We were created for greatness. We are called, by Christ's work and mercy, to display his image before the world; to love as he loved, to forgive others as he forgave us, to lay down our lives in service to others, and in our works to demonstrate the essence of value, dignity, and grace.

Cori Salchert of Sheboygan, Wisconsin, is such a minster of grace. A registered nurse with eight biological children of her own, she takes in dying infants.[2] Some of these babies are fostered. Some are adopted. Emmalynn, a baby born without either the right or left hemispheres of the brain spent her last days with Cori's family. She lived for 50 days. "Emmalynn passed away tucked into Cori's green robe, 'like a kangaroo,' while foster mother and daughter sat alone at the kitchen table one night. 'Emmalynn lived more in 50 days than most people do in a lifetime,' Cori said."[3]

Cori and her husband, Mark, show the world the value and grace of each human life. This is not the easy path. It is painful and cruelly sad. But it can bring peace to those already burdened with terrible sadness. There is a weight of dignity and love expressed in iron when we respond in love to the call of suffering. Cori understands this. The Salcherts decide as a family as each opportunity to care for a new hospice baby arises. It isn't ever easy to balance family needs with one of these special children in their lives, and making personal sacrifices becomes a part of living. One such child, Charlie, has Hypoxic Ischemic Brain Encephalopathy. "He is tracheostomy, ventilator, and tube feeding dependent among other medical challenges."[4]

But the Salchert children are learning in spite of difficult circumstances what it means to truly love. "When people ask Mark why his family has chosen to care for children with a life-limiting diagnosis and endure the emotions that come with such a situation, he tells them, 'God is love, and He loves this little boy, and He loves us to love him. Charlie is truly an amazing individual; he's made us richer –more alive in a sense.'"[5] Cori adds, "He will die; there's no changing that. But, we can make a difference

2. Ulatowski, "He's Made Us Richer," *Sheboygan Press*, 6.

3. Ulatowski, Ibid., 6.

4. Ulatowski, Ibid., 6.

5. Ulatowski, Ibid., 6.

in how he lives, and the difference for Charlie is that he will be loved before he dies."[6]

In The Trenches

1. What does it mean for Cori and Mark to walk in the good works God has prepared for them?

2. How is this walk of grace different than protesting against abortion?

Day 3

Postings from the Front

"Perhaps one of the reasons why God chooses to leave us in this terribly broken world with its various disappointments is to create in our souls a certain dissatisfaction, an insatiable hunger for home. In his sovereign plan, this world is not meant to be our final destination; we're not meant to live with a right–here, right–now mentality, where we expend our physical, emotional, spiritual, financial, and relational energies trying to turn this temporal home into the eternal home it will never be."—Paul David Tripp. [7]

In a recent *World Magazine* article, author Jae Wasson describes how seemingly random Americans are being put on ISIS hit lists. While some names might be logical by ISIS standards (soldiers, drone operators, government workers), other names seem random, strictly intended to incite terror. How do Norman and Betty, longtime missionaries, married for 51 years, respond to the news that they are now on an ISIS hit list? "'Well, I thought we were pretty safe up here in the mountains,' Betty said, and they are not concerned anyway; 'We are all on Satan's hit list and we've been on his for a long time, so what's new? We're ready to go.'"—Jae Wasson[8]

"Nearly all of our patients were young. Some of them were dying. I had reason then to be thankful for the eternal truths we had found during our meetings in the bamboo grove, for again and again my charges brought me face to face with the great basic

6. Ulatowski, Ibid., 6.

7. Tripp, Preface to *Home*, by Elyse Fitzpatrick, 10.

8. Wasson, "Sowing Fear," World Magazine, 45.

problems of human experience. Nearly all of their queries were concealed forms of the Big One; 'How do I face death? Can death be overcome?'

Reason had no more to say on this subject than 'There's nothing to life beyond the fact that we are born, we suffer and we die.' Most of us were accustomed to such an answer, for it had been stamped indelibly on our subconscious minds by the many conditioning processes of the twentieth century. This may have sufficed for normal living, but for men dying away from home in a jungle prison camp it was not enough.

When an acceptable answer was demanded of me, I had to go beyond Reason—I had to go to Faith. If I had learned to trust Jesus at all, I had to trust him here. Reason said, 'We live to die.' Jesus said, 'I am the resurrection and the life.' . . . A God who remained indifferent to the suffering of His creatures was not a God whom we could accept. The Crucifixion, however, told us that God was in our midst, suffering with us. We did not know the full answer to the mystery of suffering, but we could see that so much of it was caused by 'man's inhumanity to man', by selfishness, by greed and by all the forces of death that we readily support in the normal course of life. The cry of the innocent child, the agony I had seen in the eyes of a Chinese mother as she carried her dead baby, the suffering caused by earthquakes, fires or floods, we could not explain. But we could see that God was not indifferent to such pain . . . Faith would not save us from it, but it would take us through it."—Ernest Gordon[9]

In The Trenches

1. These readings give us a better picture of being a weak foot soldier in a broken world. What does Paul Tripp say is one of God's strategies for doing this? Why do you think we are tempted to make this world Eden?

2. Norman, Betty, and Ernest are real people. What gave these wounded warriors the confidence and hope to carry on under extremely difficult circumstances?

9. Gordon, *To End All Wars*, 119–20.

Day 4

The Threshing Floor

"I'm in the battle,"
He says,
"Winds of sad
are blowing through.
I cannot read the word.
My eye is restless,
Roaming,
Never seeing,
Blind to light.
Oh, where is He who rescues me?"

"My vision is a sorrow.
Cataracts of pain
have muted
all the vibrant colors in my life.
Distorting joy,
Reducing blues and greens
to yellowed browns.
Like aged and faded paper
I am past,
Forgotten,
And my heart a brittle lens,
A wall between
my sight and His.
I cannot see.
But God Who Sees,
Sees me."

"I'm in the battle,"
He says,
"Winds of sad
are blowing through.
I cannot hear Him speak to me.

The word is jumbled,
Empty consonants and vowels,
Sounds without a meaning.
I am wailing,
Crying,
Deaf to hoping.
Oh, where is He who rescues me?
All I hear is silence.
Shame and sin
Have muzzled
all the joy and laughter in my life,
Distracting me from grace,
From peace,
From everything that lifts my soul.
And so I fall.
I flounder,
I am falling into empty space,
Unfulfilled,
Alone,
Vacuum between heart and Him.
I cannot hear.
But He Who Hears,
Hears me."

"I'm in the battle,"
He says,
"Winds of sad
are blowing through.
I do not have the strength to dress,
The energy to rise each day.
Somehow the distance
spans a thousand miles,
A vast eternity
between my bed and life.
Preventing me
from leaving sheets and blankets
here behind.

Instead they bind,
They are my shroud of lethargy.
Oh, where is He who rescues me?"

The Christ Who Stands,
He stands with me.
He bore my pain.
He took my sin
And wore my shame.
He took it all,
And bound His life to human shroud
to pay my debt.
I hear the wind,
I see the chaff fly clean away.
I know His battle swallows mine.
This pain,
This sad
that rends my core,
Was carried first,
Was laid on Him before
I ever crossed the threshing floor.

In The Trenches

1. The threshing floor is a level, hard surface where the harvested sheaves of grain are placed to separate the good grain from the useless, tough husks. In Bible times, oxen and cattle were walked repeatedly over the sheaves to loosen the husks from the grain. Sometimes people used sticks to pound the sheaves. How does the poem compare our battle with suffering, sin, and the enemy, to a threshing floor?

2. The Bible also used the threshing floor as a metaphor of God's judgement. Why does Christ give us hope on the threshing floor?

Day 5

Heart Check

"Have this mind among yourselves, which is yours in Christ Jesus, who, though he was in the form of God, did not count equality with God a thing to be grasped, but made himself nothing, taking the form of a servant, being born in the likeness of men. And being found in human form, he humbled himself by becoming obedient to the point of death, even death on a cross" (Phil 2:5–8).

How can we walk with determination and love when the road is paved with pain and suffering?

Love Unbound

The shadows fall.
The cup is passed.
My shame is bound to Him.

He bleeds!
He bleeds!
It is my sin that holds Him fast!

Can't look at Him.
Can't be with Him.
Can't breathe His air.
Why does He care so much for me?

It is His love
That makes Him grasp the tree
and not let go.
It is His love
that holds Him there.

He does not turn away,
And He who gulps my precious air
has swallowed all,
My striving,
All my blame.

"I thirst," He said.
And here I am,
The thirsty one,
The one who hungers to be fed.

Week 28–Overcome Me by Holy Fire

Day 1

Studying the Battle Plan

"It is for discipline that you have to endure. God is treating you as sons. For what son is there whom his father does not discipline? If you are left without discipline, in which all have participated, then you are illegitimate children and not sons. Besides this, we have had earthly fathers who disciplined us and we respected them. Shall we not much more be subject to the Father of spirits and live? For they disciplined us for a short time as it seemed best to them, but he disciplines us for our good, that we may share his holiness. For the moment all discipline seems painful rather than pleasant, but later it yields the peaceful fruit of righteousness to those who have been trained by it" (Heb 12:7–11).

In The Trenches

1. Some battles are more difficult than others. Some take up our whole life. How are we to view these kinds of battles?

2. What does this passage tell us about God's love?

Day 2

Scouting the Territory

At the age of sixteen, I watched my grandmother disappear. Her mind had been slipping into forgetfulness for a couple of years. First it was dates and names, and then it was how to warm a can of soup. She was moving away at lightning speed; faster than her body was aging. She could still eat pizza in her eighties, but couldn't remember her sons. She couldn't keep track of her teeth soaking in the glass next to her bed, but she greeted all visitors with the graciousness, elegance, and gentle humor that had been one of her glories all of her life. I saw others of her age and infirmity that were not only lost in time, but lost in soul; men and women who cried and screamed against their own growing darkness; impatient, lonely people wandering the halls in confusion. It made an enormous impression on my young heart.

Now I realize that some dispositions that afflict those with dementia are beyond the control of those who suffer. A sweet woman can turn into a bitter and sour old lady and it is the disease that is causing it. But as I watched my grandmother and her kind disposition, I asked God to make me like her if my mind would someday fly away. Somehow God had preserved his grace and glory in this woman–child who greeted us each week.

A sixteen–year–old girl does not realize what she is asking. It was a proper prayer. But we humans are not born with such graces. They are welded into us through holy fire. I know this now, and my grandmother knew it at some level, because her life had been offered up to Christ's grace long ago. His own wise, yet unfathomable workings were recreating her through trials: a husband sent to sea in war time, a child who died, loss of job and security during the Depression, the heartache and worry that went with her husband's five heart attacks and eventual death from cancer. But the fire also gave her a firm grip on Christ, and the confidence that he had an even greater grip on her. She used to read to me from her well–worn Bible, quoting in both English and French. I saw her Bible. It was filled with scribbled notes, comments, and prayers. She knew this Christ on a very intimate level, and he made a difference in her life. She talked about a happy and fulfilled life with her husband and sons. She shared favorite hymns, and memories of summer Bible conferences. She showed me a life lived for Christ can be one of grace as well as pain.

I know this because Christ has been faithfully answering my teenage prayer. I, too, have been, and continue to be in his fire. It burns, and he has given me a life marked by great difficulties and sorrows. But his fire draws me to him; to his love, his strength, his grace, his hope. And I am being transformed by it. I am at sixty-two a far different woman than I was at sixteen; not perfect by any means, but surely kinder, more understanding, and loving. It is his gift. And if I too become one of those lost in time, I still pray that I will express his character whether I know it or not. And if such a disease turns my song sour, I pray that he will be glorified despite my outward countenance; that his inner grace will somehow show through.

In The Trenches

1. What might it mean to offer your life totally over to God, and be given a difficult gift?

2. Do our lives glorify God in spite of our difficult gift, or because of that gift?

Day 3

Postings from the Front

"Lars Gren led me down a dim hallway to a simple room lit magnificently by floor–to–ceiling windows that looked out over the Atlantic Ocean. A slim, elderly woman dressed in black pants and a floral shirt—her hair swirled in a bun—sat near the fireplace. 'We have company today,' Gren said, bending down to touch her hand. His wife, Elisabeth Elliot, nodded but did not reply.

Since the onset of dementia about a decade ago, the best–selling and widely known Christian author communicates mostly through slight hand gestures and facial expressions. For everything else, there's Lars Gren, her husband of thirty-six years. He and two caregivers attend to her daily needs. He answers letters, manages ministry orders, and updates 'Ramblings from the Cove,' a blog about their doings . . .

Elliot stopped giving speeches in 2004 as her health worsened. When she realized she was losing her memory, she put into practice what she had long preached: 'From acceptance comes peace.' Her husband said she turned to the Bible for comfort, especially Isaiah 43:2: 'When you pass through the waters, I will be with you; and through the rivers, they shall not overwhelm you; when you walk through the fire, you shall not be burned, and the flame shall not consume you.'

Gren says Elliot has handled dementia just as she did the deaths of her husbands. 'She accepted those things, [knowing] they were no surprise to God,' Gren said. 'It was something she would rather not have experienced, but she received it.'

Hearing these words, Elliot looked up and nodded, her eyes clear and strong. Then she spoke for the first time during the two–hour interview, nodding vigorously: 'Yes.'"—Tiffany Owens[1]

"So we do not lose heart. Though our outer self is wasting away, our inner self is being renewed day by day. For this light momentary affliction is preparing for us an eternal weight of glory beyond all comparison, as we look not to the things that are seen but to the things that are unseen. For the things that are seen are transient, but the things that are unseen are eternal" (2 Cor 4:16–18).

In The Trenches

1. How did Elisabeth Elliot respond to God's gift of dementia?

2. What does God promise to those who offer their lives to him?

Day 4

For a Friend with Alzheimer's

Don't forget me, Lord, when I forget.
Remember my name.

My mind slips,

---

1. Owens, "Walking Through Fire," World Magazine, 57–8.

Slides,
I can't remember what you said.
The answer hides.

Lord, give me friends who listen
when I ask again.

My mind remembers one thought
whispered over and over,
It lingers,
Caught.
Lord give me friends who revel in the present
when I speak again.

My mind is fragile,
Traveling like an Escher picture–
Up and down to nowhere.
Thoughts disconnected.
Once was agile,
Lost somewhere.

Don't lose me Lord, when I am lost.
I try again.
Don't forget me, Lord, when I forget.
Remember my name.

I Miss You, Friend

I miss you, friend.
You may be near,
Warm fingers touching mine.

Alas,
I find your mind has closed
to what we shared together.
Dates and memories are packed and sealed,
Such thoughts congealed,
Forgotten.

Only Now remains to be explored.

This rank disease has stolen you
and left this stranger
sitting here across from me.
You might as well be miles away,
An ocean of confusion
Filling space between us,
Washing recollection off the floor.

To you I am a continent,
Unknown,
Unknowable,
Vast and graying on a far horizon,
Far,
Too far to recognize,
A shadow on a distant shore.

I am alone.
And yet we touch,
We hug,
We sit together.
Two lost souls,
One memory gone,
One holding on and wanting more.
I miss you, friend.

In The Trenches

1. Read Isaiah 49:14–16. Will God ever forget us even if we can't remember him?

2. Read 2 Corinthians 5:1. What do we have confidence in that gives us courage in difficult times?

Day 5

Heart Check

I have a close friend who is losing her battle with Alzheimer's. I have another dear friend who is fading into old age; struggling with constant and debilitating pain issues and exhaustion after simple activities. Little by little, they are losing their ability to take care of themselves. Their bodies are betraying them, but their hearts are free to worship, to find deep joy in modest daily tasks and in friendships. Their bodies no longer skip and run, but their hearts soar. Because Alzheimer's keeps your mind always in the present, my friend is always ready to worship and serve her King. She has no fear of the future. The friend in pain has been given great gifts of endurance and wisdom. She is a wise friend to others. She is committed to prayer.

God has not promised a life free of illness or pain, but a full and satisfying life, a productive life when we live in Christ. Do you see old age or Alzheimer's, or cancer, as end games, or other opportunities to find new ways to love and serve Christ more?

Week 29—Is He Enough?

Day 1

Studying the Battle Plan

"For God alone, O my soul, wait in silence. For my hope is from him. He only is my rock and my salvation, my fortress; I shall not be shaken. On God rests my salvation and my glory; my mighty rock, my refuge is God. Trust in him at all times, O people; pour out your heart before him; God is a refuge for us" (Ps 62:5–8).

In The Trenches

1. What does it mean to truly trust God?
2. When you think of your life, what does it mean to endure?

Day 2

Scouting the Territory

When my granddaughter was three years old, she never went anywhere without "The Two"—a pair of extremely worn, and much loved, matching, brown teddy bears. They were her constant companions. One afternoon, in a hurry to get some errands done, her parents quickly packed her and her older brother into their car seats. As Daddy backed out of the driveway, there was a panicked wail from the backseat. "The Two! Daddy, I don't have The Two! I can't manage without The Two!"

I can't manage. It doesn't matter who you are or what the circumstances. We all have those can't manage moments—bad traffic or car trouble on a day the schedule counts the most, feeling overwhelmed and underqualified by a child's needs or behavior, a medical diagnosis that brings all our plans for the future to a screeching halt. From transient annoyances all the way to facing a "new normal," in each instance we are thrown in that moment from feeling firmly in control to helplessness. It seems counterintuitive to say this, but it is the best place we could be. God, in his infinite wisdom, has put you in the position to look up, to trust in him, to tune your heart to Jesus through the power of the Holy Spirit that has been at work in you all along.

In John 14–16, Jesus has been preparing his disciples for his coming betrayal and death, his resurrection, and his return to glory. He is talking about leaving. "I will not leave you as orphans," (John 14:18) he says. "You will weep and lament . . . You will be sorrowful, but your sorrow will turn to joy" (John 16:20). Jesus is about to enter into the great battle; the battle that empties The Dragon of the power to accuse and destroy. He sees what they cannot see. There will be battles ahead for them as well as they begin their life's work, the work he has prepared them for, to bring the gospel to the nations. "They will put you out of the synagogues. Indeed the hour is coming when whoever kills you will think he is offering service to God. And they will do these things because they have not known the Father, nor me. But I have said these things to you, that when their hour comes you may remember that I told them to you" (John 16:2–4).

Christ's command is simple. "If anyone loves me, he will keep my word." Love and obey. How is this simple? The disciples will all hide after the cross. I still fight my fears. Somehow we are all back at "I can't manage." But Christ already had a solution to daily battles with fear, with doubt, and with weakness—the Holy Spirit. "And I will ask the Father, and he will give you another Helper, to be with you forever, even the Spirit of truth, whom the world cannot receive, because it neither sees him nor knows him. You know him, for he dwells with you and will be in you" (John14:16–17). Jesus calls the Holy Spirit the *parakletos*, usually translated as counselor (as in legal advocate), comforter, or helper. It means, "one who is called alongside," "to encourage," "to exhort."[1] He knows we cannot do what he has commanded of us unless we have the help of the third person of the Trinity. It is the Holy Spirit that convicts us and others of sin. It is the Holy Spirit that speaks Jesus and his word into our hearts and gives us understanding.

1. Carson, *Gospel According to John*, 499.

It is the Holy Spirit that teaches us what love and obedience really mean. It is the Holy Spirit who dwells with us, who empowers us to complete the work he has already planned for us. It is the Holy Spirit who intercedes for us in our prayers. It is only by the indwelling working of the Holy Spirit that we manage at all. It is the Spirit that arms us for our daily battles. He prepares us to walk alongside each other, to serve one another. He is there to apply Jesus' work in us to our attitudes, our actions, and our words. Paul tells us in Romans 8:26 that the Spirit helps us in our weakness. And it is the Holy Spirit, states Ephesians 1:13, that marks us forever as belonging to Christ, who guarantees our inheritance. The ESV note renders it "until God redeems his possession,"[2] until he gathers us to our share in his eternal kingdom, and we, his treasured possession, are finally taken home.

In my own battles, I realized today that the question in my mind was not: "Is this all true?" but that my heart keeps asking, "Is he enough?" When the battle is all around me, I falter because I see how weak and small I am. I am three again, like my granddaughter, hoping in teddy bears. I know the resurrection from the dead is Christ's ultimate sign. It shouts, "Everything he said is true!" It energizes, provides direction, purpose, and hope. But it is not Christ's resurrection from the dead and his promises that make me waver. It is day by day living with a weak nature in a fallen world. When you are three, two trusted teddy bears and a daddy that lovingly rushes back into the house to bring them to you is enough. But I need more than teddy bears. I need a Father who will love and carry me all the way to the grave. It is a matter of a trusting heart, even in the face of illness and sorrow. It is faith in the Man/God that carries me through the battle. Hebrews says that "Faith is the assurance [the substance and reality] of things hoped for, the conviction [or evidence] of things not seen" (Heb 11:1). I am trusting in Christ, and he has promised to be with me all the way to the end.

So I ask myself—am I trusting that he who began a good work in me will complete it? He has promised he will. Has my life been guided by the Holy Spirit's unpacking of the word to my heart, and by the lives of others he has sent to live grace and mercy before me? Has it been guided by his kindness and comfort when I needed it most? "Yes," I say, looking back on sixty-two years, and a thousand memories of holy rescue; on the words of Scripture being burned into my mind and played out in my life; on the Comforter faithfully witnessing Christ's work and word and wrestling it into my heart. Yes, he is enough.

2. ESV Study footnote, 2263.

In The Trenches

1. Do you find yourself asking if God is enough for you in your struggles?

2. How can you know for sure you will have the strength and fortitude to keep going no matter what?

3. Read Galatians 2:20; Philippians 1:21. What does it mean "to live is Christ?"

Day 3

In Honor of Esther

He always held her up.
He never let her go.
It didn't matter whether
Loss of sight
Or fading heart
became the center of her day.
He carried her
with loving hands along the way,
His path of most resistance.

She who walked with all the pain,
Her limitations all considered loss
for greater gain,
She told me
Even cancer could not mar the Glory Road.

For every scar,
Each aching weakness
Came as Holy gifts from Him,
Her body branded by His love,
Her suffering with gentle grace
a grand display of His embrace.
No ache too hard to take,
No need to hide,
As long as He be glorified.

In The Trenches

1. Read Philippians 1:21

2. How did Esther exemplify Philippians 1:21?

Day 4

Masks and Other Paper

Sometimes I feel like window dressing,
Pretty folded paper
decorating life.
No weight attached
to give me depth.
Just fluff.

Too fragile in the aftermath
of struggles piling on
to be much strength or fortitude,
But only pictures,
Symbols of what should be there but isn't.

How unfair.

I'd like to be just what I seem,
More underneath,
More firm foundation
matching what is out in front,
Quite on display.
More real,
As I was meant to be.

I worry that the hostile breezes
flowing through
might unmask what you cannot see.
But I keep moving forward,
Knowing He

Somehow,
Some way,
Is really undergirding this old paper peacock.
Deep inside these iridescent feathers
pumps a lion's heart.
Not mine, but His.
He carries, lifts,
Revives, rebuilds.
And, recreating,
Morphs old paper into steel,
An origami braced with wire
Molding strength.

So when the fires of this world
Come roaring through,
Beneath the ash of fluff reveals
His own remains,
The shape of Life
traced out in me.

Sometimes I feel like window dressing,
Pretty folded paper
Decorating life.

How grateful folded paper,
Can be folded into Christ!
His life,
His weight,
His gravitas sustaining me
through daily strife.
His lion heart
beats firmly,
Synchronizing window dressing
into grand design.
Still paper,
Yet His strength envelops mine.

In The Trenches

1. What does it mean in this poem to be a mask or a piece of paper? Do you ever feel the same way?

2. How is the speaker able to overcome? Where do you go when you think you are only paper?

Day 5

Heart Check

"And my God will supply every need of yours according to his riches in glory in Christ Jesus" (Phil 4:19).

Do you know this to be true? How does knowing this help you move forward in dark and difficult moments?

Week 30–Truly Safe

Day 1

Studying the Battle Plan

"Do not lay up for yourselves treasures on earth, where moth and rust destroy and where thieves break in and steal, but lay up for yourselves treasures in heaven, where neither moth nor rust destroys and where thieves do not break in and steal. For where your treasure is, there you heart will be also" (Matt 6:19–21).

In The Trenches

1. What is intended to be our highest treasure?
2. What does what your treasure say about your heart?

Day 2

Scouting the Territory

As small children, most of us tethered ourselves to security blankets and teddy bears. We seemed to sense that the world is a dangerous place, requiring some intimate and trustworthy coping skills on our part, something outside of ourselves to help us face the day. Of course, we might have trusted in parents, truly grand and powerful beings to a young child's mind. But teddy bears and blankets expressed our acute separateness: that being finite in many ways is to be alone, hence the reassuring warm and familiar blanket. One of my sons called his teddy his "nightmare exterminator." I think that eloquently sums it up.

I remember when my younger sister, Sheila, was standing at the door, ready to step out of the house and into her new adventure with kindergarten. She had her shiny new lunchbox in one hand, but she also had her blanket grasped firmly in the other hand, its warm and comforting fuzziness pressed to her chest. My father said, "It's either the blanket or kindergarten. You can't do both." She looked at the door. She looked at the blanket. The door. The blanket. Suddenly she threw the blanket down and marched out into the rest of her life.

I think we believe that when we, as little children, threw our blankets down, we were confidently walking away from our childish fears for safety and security. We were moving forward; growing up into adult life, no longer requiring teddy bears and security blankets. If we think that way we are fooling ourselves. Our whole life is about how finite and separate we know we are. We search for connections with each other because we know we are alone. And we replace our teddy bears with adult versions of security: a comfortable home, extra money in the bank. We build routines into our lives that give us illusions of safety and control. We still want to be safe. What we need is to be saved. We are all needy, fragile beings in a huge universe. We know it. We fight it. But we can't quite get away from it, because we are not only alone, we are alone in our sin. We are imperfect, inconsistent, and rebellious. We want all that this world offers our way, even though our way is messy, imperfect, lonely, and often burdened.

Jesus Christ offers a truly comprehensive salvation, but it is not the promise of safety. It is the promise of rest and release from our sinful impulses and actions. This translates into rest from the burdens we impose on ourselves by our fears, our failures, and even our successes. Jesus asks us to let go of us, and all the things we depend on, and follow him (Matt 11:28–29). "Take my perfect life," he tells us, "and drop off your restless and wayward thoughts, your feeble works, your boasting pride, your loneliness, your struggle to love and be loved, your flooding doubts and moments of emptiness. Throw down all that you think will give you security, safety, and peace. Wear me," he is saying, "for I am gentle and lowly in heart, and you will find rest for your souls. I swallowed all your darkness, your fears, and your shame, at the cross. Wear me because I already carried all the terrible weight of you. I wore it. I destroyed it with my blood. It's gone. Wear me instead. For my yoke is easy, and my burden is light." You don't need to be safe from this world. You need to be safe from yourself and your sin.

Sheila was swallowed up by Life in 2002, entering into the presence of Jesus for all eternity. When her husband and my parents were sorting through her forty–plus years of personal treasures, they discovered a small, worn square of blanket. It was a bittersweet reminder of our frailty in this life, our constant need to lean on our Savior, and the sweetness and love of his grace. He knows, he understands, and he loves us all the way through.

In The Trenches

1. What is the difference between being safe and saved? Why is it so important?

2. Do you treasure your salvation?

3. What does it mean to "wear Christ?"

Day 3

Pray for Grace

Aptly named,
She mends the day
with reverence and prayer,
Each hour a happening,
A crisis borne
of childish care—
The baby cries,
His older siblings vie and pout,
Their elbowing and strutting shouts for mother's time.

And then there's that one child
Who faces life another way,
A slower,
Sometimes upside display,
Sometimes perverse reminder
That one misplaced DNA

Forever reconstructs an expectation
into mazes,
Different roads and pleasures
Changing human downs and spills to ups,
And rearranging even, solid ground
To massive hills and water spouts.

And Grace grows wearied
by the constancy of swallowing life,
While she is fighting its disorder,
Sweeping crumbs,
(The constant flow an endless crust),
And gathering toys and socks
that dust and decorate incessant stairs.
Pray for Grace.

It's hard sometimes to give a smile,
A softer word,
A gentle space.
So she keeps mending,
Praying for her children's hearts,
Her own,
Her husband,
Always busy someplace else,
And all the myriad of family members
Offering up their own advice:
"Be kind."
"Be strict."
"If they were my kids"—
But they aren't.
They're hers, not yours.

And she has chores and callings
You can't possibly conceive or comprehend.
Where you have order,
She has floors—
Untidy, mounds of racing life.
Where you have structure,

She has doors
that take her into joy and strife.
Where you have quiet,
She has stores
of noisy wonders and confusions,
Working out each day decisions
never thought about before.
But she keeps mending,
Sending all her cries and needs before the LORD.
And you, too,
Could become an answer,
Someone side by side
In tandem,
Worshipping before the throne.
Pray for grace.

In The Trenches

1. The mother in this poem cannot choose being safe. She has been given a holy gift filled with risks and struggles. What is it like to be her? To live in her world?

2. What are her heart's treasures?

Day 4

Studying the Battle Plan

"Indeed, I count everything as loss because of the surpassing worth of knowing Christ Jesus my Lord. For his sake I have suffered the loss of all things and count them as rubbish, in order that I may gain Christ and be found in him, not having a righteousness of my own that comes from the law, but that which comes through faith in Christ, the righteousness from God that depends on faith—that I may know him and the power of his resurrection, and may share his sufferings, becoming like him in his death, that by any means possible I may attain the resurrection from the dead.

Not that I have already obtained this or am already perfect, but I press on to make it my own, because Christ Jesus has made me his own. Brothers, I do not consider that I have made it my own. But one thing I do: forgetting what lies behind and straining forward to what lies ahead, I press on toward the goal for the prize of the upward call of God in Christ Jesus" (Phil 3:8–14).

In The Trenches

1. Who is in charge of Paul's life?
2. What does it mean to "press on?"

Day 5

Heart Check

"A mighty fortress is our God, a bulwark never failing;
Our helper he amid the flood of mortal ills prevailing.
For still our ancient foe doth seek to work us woe;
His craft and pow'r are great;
And armed with cruel hate,
On earth is not his equal.

Did we in our own strength confide, our striving would be losing;
Were not the right man on our side, the man of God's own choosing.
Dost ask who that may be? Christ Jesus, it is he,
Lord Sabaoth his name,
From age to age the same,
And he must win the battle.

And though this world, with devils filled, should threaten to undo us,
We will not fear, for God hath willed his truth to triumph through us.
The prince of darkness grim, we tremble not for him;
His rage we can endure,
For lo! his doom is sure;
One little word shall fell him.

That Word above all earthly pow'rs, no thanks to them, abideth.

The Spirit and the gifts are ours through him who with us sideth.
Let goods and kindred go, this mortal life also;
The body they may kill:
God's truth abideth still;
His kingdom is forever."[1]

1. How are we to face the troubles and cares of this life?

2. How many of God's promises can you find in this hymn?

---

1. Luther, *Trinity Hymnal*, 92.

Week 31—Consuming Love

Day 1

Studying the Battle Plan

"Shadrach, Meshach, and Abednego answered and said to the king, 'O Nebuchadnezzar, we have no need to answer you in this matter. If this be so, our God whom we serve is able to deliver us from the burning fiery furnace, and he will deliver us out of your hand, O king. But if not, be it known to you, O king, that we will not serve your gods or worship the golden image that you have set up.'

Then Nebuchadnezzar was filled with fury, and the expression of his face was changed against Shadrach, Meshach, and Abednego. He ordered the furnace heated seven times more than it was usually heated. And he ordered some of the mighty men of his army to bind Shadrach, Meshach, and Abednego, and to cast them into the burning fiery furnace. Then these men were bound in their cloaks, their tunics, their hats, and their other garments, and they were thrown into the burning fiery furnace. Because the king's order was urgent and the furnace overheated, the flame of the fire killed those men who took up Shadrach, Meshach, and Abednego. And these three men, Shadrach, Meshach, and Abednego, fell bound into the burning fiery furnace.

Then King Nebuchadnezzar was astonished and rose up in haste. He declared to his counselors, 'Did we not cast three men bound into the fire?' They answered and said to the king, 'True, O king.' He answered and said, 'But I see four men unbound, walking in the midst of the fire, and they are not hurt, and the appearance of the fourth is like a son of the gods'" (Dan 3:16–25).

In The Trenches

1. What did it mean for Shadrach, Meshach, and Abednego to choose God over the safe path?

2. Of whom were they more afraid?

Day 2

Scouting the Territory

God is love. It is often the first truth we learn as toddlers in Sunday school. We would like it to be the love of a comfortable, loving, and indulgent father. Such a deity might be easily appeased and manipulated. He could certainly be ignored. This God cannot. His love is both undeserved and unconditionally and graciously offered to the perpetually undeserving. His love is gritty and raw. Christ, the Son, gave up the throne of heaven to live among us, to know our weakness, yet was without sin. He died a hideously gruesome death on our behalf, and then overcame our worst enemy, death, in his glorious resurrection. "For one will scarcely die for a righteous person— though perhaps for a good person one would dare even to die—but God shows his love for us in that while we were still sinners, Christ died for us" (Rom 5:7–8). This is love that demands both our attention and our adoration.

But God is also just. God, speaking to Israel through Moses in Deuteronomy 32:20–22, calls down judgment in the face of Israel's apostasy. "And he said, 'I will hide my face from them; I will see what their end will be, for they are a perverse generation, children in whom is no faithfulness. They have made me jealous with what is no god; they have provoked me to anger with their idols. So I will make them jealous with those who are no people; I will provoke them to anger with a foolish nation. For a fire is kindled by my anger, and it burns to the depths of Sheol, devours the earth and its increase, and sets on fire the foundations of the mountains.'"

God is a consuming fire. He was a consuming fire before his people in the wilderness, and at Mount Sinai (Deut 4:24, 5:24–25). He is still a consuming fire today (Hebrews 12:29).

Not exactly the kind of God twenty-first century Western society is looking for. We like the idea of that indulgent, manageable, old father. But we need a God who is both loving and just, both merciful, and a consuming fire. Just ask Shadrach, Meshach, and Abednego. They have been commanded, by law, to worship an idol; to choose between worshipping the one true God, and certain death. They are not confused by diluted mush about "God would never let that happen to me. He's a God of love." They know he is capable of destroying them without the help of Nebuchadnezzer. They come from a long line of ancestors with a history of rebellion; a stiff–necked people undeserving of rescue that goes all the way back to Adam and Eve and the forbidden fruit. They may individually strive to serve God as he commands, but they are part of the larger community; Israel, a nation exiled to this foreign court because of their rebellion. These faithful men have no delusions that belonging to the right God protects them from suffering and pain.

But they also know the Lord, their covenant King, has declared himself to be a God of mercy (Exod 34:6–7a). They are waiting, putting their very lives on the line. They are declaring their faith in the one promised, their hope in the Messiah yet to come. They are showing confident assurance in the God who will someday show mercy to the unjust by raining his justice on the merciful Son. And so they bravely tell the mighty king of Babylon, "our God, whom we serve is able to deliver us from the burning fiery furnace and he will deliver us out of your hand, O king. But if not, be it known to you, O king, that we will not serve your gods or worship the golden image that you have set up" (Dan 3:17–18). They assume they will die. But they would rather stand in awe of the consuming fire of God than fear the fiery furnace of man.

Their witness echoes in the persecuted church right now facing unspeakable things: beheadings, being burned alive, imprisonment, torture, persecution, starvation, exile from homes and livelihoods. Our hearts should burn in prayer for those suffering in the raging fires set before them. Their stance of trust under fire should be ours as well. We may not be currently experiencing the horrors facing our brothers and sisters, but we are all just one day, one hour, or one step away from a situation beyond our control; anything that turns our world upside down, and threatens our theology.

When your world catches fire, do you really believe what you recite on Sunday morning or read in your daily devotionals? Do you trust in God's magnificent love, a God with us love that went all the way to the cross? And are you resting in the promise that this God is also just, and will bring justice to all who cry out for it now, but do not yet see it? Are you assured that Christ is enough—enough love, enough justice, enough power, to faithfully bring his people through each and every day, and someday usher us into his promised restoration, his glorious and forever holy kingdom?

Shadrach, Meshach, and Abednego get it. They are a literal picture of faith under fire, bound and thrown into the midst of the howling furnace. Daniel has included the fact that the burly men sent to throw these three believers to their death are destroyed by the blaze themselves. Why is this information so important? It underlines the fact that the fiery furnace was real. It was fierce and deadly. But in this terrible ordeal we see hope. There are not three men in the fire, but four. God is among them! We do not know if this is a physical appearance of Christ before his incarnation, or one of God's angels. We do know that they walk in the fire but are not burned. God's presence is so comprehensive that there isn't even the smell of smoke on their clothes or bodies when they emerge from the furnace (Dan 3:24–27). They live because they put their faith in the consuming fire of God. We who belong to God and are under suffering, also stand within the consuming fire. And like Shadrach, Meshach, and Abednego, we do not stand alone, and we are not consumed. The God of Sinai's consuming fire that destroys is also the God that covered us with the sprinkled blood of Christ. He is in the fire with us, and will walk us all the way through to the end. Love has met justice, and the acrid odor of this world's worst smoke can never touch us.

In The Trenches

1. What kind of God do we serve?

2. Why do we need such a God?

Day 3

Endurance Road

So this is what the road of Grace demands,
A walking strewn with sorrows,
Vast uncertainties,
Rough–hewn places
Carving ruts of pain,
Deep pain and miseries.
Like steel within the furnace,
I am filled with fire.
Those who stand beside me smell the smoke.

I do not taste the flame,
For He Who Walks Beside Me
Bore the burning for my sake,
And I am free.

Still wandering through the haze,
Inferno blazing high about my every move,
The pain sears every step
But I remain undaunted,
Still enduring,
Knowing He Who Walks is holding me,
Is still beside me,
Turning chaff to ash and flinging it away,
His holding changing inconsistencies and imperfections into gain.

In The Trenches

1. Why do you think the speaker calls the Christian life the endurance road?

2. Why do you think she still chooses it even though it is painful and not safe?

Day 4

A Dialogue with Pain

O LORD,
My legs are weary,
Aching,
Trembling under weight and pain,
I cannot stand.

Dear Child,
Let me be legs for you.
For I,
Who did not think equality with God
a thing to grasp,
But walked instead
The road of sorrows to the Cross,
And claimed the lowest place
Before the face of God
on your behalf,
I drank your dregs.
I died your death.
And even angel hosts must bow,
Must fall before my gory head.

O LORD,
My arms are useless,
Lost appendages.
I cannot even lift them up to pray.

Dear Child,
Let me be arms for you.
For I
Who did not enter holy places made with hands,
But claimed the heavenly space
before the face of God
on your behalf,
I reach for you.

I pray for you.
And even searing stars must weep,
Must bow if I command.

O LORD,
My tongue is quarrels,
Burning,
Raging,
Staining heart and soul.
I vacillate from hot to cold.
I should not speak.

Dear Child,
Let me be mouth for you.
For I
Who said "Let there be light!"
And so it was,
And it was good.
Who made all things,
The Light that darkness can't contain,
I called your name.
I made you mine,
I raised you higher,
High above where even hell can't overwhelm,
Can't make you bow.
My Word is sure,
Secured in blood.
And Satan falls before my fire.

O LORD,
My heart goes back and forth,
From light to gray.
It wanders,
Searching,
Seething,
Sometimes wasting under sadness all the day,
And I,
A changing creature,

Am alone.

Dear Child,
Let me be heart for you.
For I am never changing,
Yesterday, today, and to forever
I am still the same.
For I,
Who laid the earth's foundations,
One day,
I will call an end to sadness,
End to pain and suffering.
I will roll them up like useless garments.
Thrown away,
They'll drop like stone,
Their memories cold,
Forgotten,
Gone.
And even soaring mountains
Must bow down before my coming,
Earth and heaven giving way before the King.
Yet even now my heart is yours.
And you, My Child,
You are forever,
Safe,
At rest.
You are my peace,
No more bereft.
Your heart resides by heaven's throne.

In The Trenches

1. What comfort does God's word give people on the endurance road?
2. What do we learn about God?

Day 5

Heart Check

"For we do not have a high priest who is unable to sympathize with our weaknesses, but one who in every respect has been tempted as we are, yet without sin. Let us then with confidence draw near to the throne of grace, that we may receive mercy and find grace to help in time of need" (Heb 4:15–16).

Can you rest on such a wondrous, powerful and sovereignly majestic God and on his direction for you? Even when you are sure you know a better way?

Week 32—Lost and Found

Day 1

Studying the Battle Plan

"How lovely is your dwelling place, O LORD of hosts! My soul longs, yes, faints for the courts of the LORD; my heart and flesh sing for joy to the living God." (Ps 84:1–2)

"And I heard a loud voice from the throne saying, 'Behold, the dwelling place of God is with man. He will dwell with them, and they will be his people, and God himself will be with them as their God. He will wipe away every tear from their eyes, and death shall be no more, neither shall there be mourning, nor crying, nor pain anymore, for the former things have passed away.'" (Rev 21:3–4)

In The Trenches

1. Do you hear the longing to be in God's presence? The longing for heaven?

2. What has God told us about heaven in Revelation 21?

Day 2

Scouting the Territory

I lost a friend a few days ago to cancer. When I say, "lost," I mean she is lost to me. I can't talk to her, can't hear her laugh, or enjoy her presence. There is a void, an emptiness in my life that is acute right now. It is as if the sun is refusing to shine on me. I know from experience that such feelings will become a dull ache over time, but won't completely go away. The acuteness, the dullness that follows, and the forever feeling are all natural consequences of love. It is part of being human.

The wonder of her death is that she is not really lost. She has been on a trajectory of being found all her life. She stopped being spiritually dead a long time ago, being made alive through the life, the death, and the resurrection of Christ. This latest trial just ends her time as a foot soldier. No more battles. No more personal struggles, no sorrows, no daily fights with pain and the constant onslaught of greater and greater diminishing returns on a body no longer interested in the war. She never stopped being interested in living for her Savior; and yet, at the same time, eagerly leaned towards heaven. Pain and endless procedures may sideline, but they cannot conquer either heart or soul. The mad hunger for something better has finally become a satisfying and full reality for her. God has taken her off the battlefield, and sent her home, where she has found rest and peace in his presence.

Someday she will be made alive again; physically alive. And this time without any fears of diminishing returns. This time will be forever. She is not lost. She is forever found. She is free.

In The Trenches

1. What do I mean when I say the words, "lost a friend?"
2. What will it mean someday for all of us to be "forever found?"

Day 3

Fixer Upper

She was destroyed by bites,
And her own earthly husband
Had to pay for her destruction.

Therapies that didn't hold,
Tests,
And possibilities that shriveled hope.

Such is disease
And its despair.
It shows no quarter,
No regrets,
But takes away,
And does not turn or take a care.

But peeling back this layered death,
See Life beneath.
Beneath the bites
See letting go of earthly loves.
See Resurrection Light
Come creeping,
Growing,
Undermining weak foundations,
Underneath like so much morning glory vines,
Their tensiled,
Gleaming tendrils
Owning,
Breaking up life only meant
for crumbling walls and settled dust.

Old house,
Old folly,
All demolished,
Shuttered down

To make a way
As old bursts tumbling into New.

She is dismantled bite by bite,
But Christ had paid for her,
His reconstruction,
Costly,
Caring,
Emptying Himself of Grace and Glory
for her care.
God showed no quarter on His Son,
And in return
He took away her last despair.

Saying Goodbye

He says goodbye a hundred times a day,
And she just lays there,
Placed there by her Heavenly Father,
Wavering between God's world and theirs.

While in his world her life is shutting down.
She cannot stay much longer.
Grace has gently held her back for his goodbyes.
But soon the letting go is greater Grace for man and wife.
For she must reach to take Love's hand,
And human love must lean and rest on His command,
Must let her fly,
Must let what dies become what lives,
Must wait.
And while he waits,
Must say goodbye.

In The Trenches

1. What kinds of grace are being created out of her disease?

2. Why is it greater grace to let go of this life and say goodbye?

Day 4

Studying the Battle Plan

"In him we have obtained an inheritance, having been predestined according to the purpose of him who works all things according to the counsel of his will, so that we who were the first to hope in Christ might be to the praise of his glory. In him you also, when you heard the word of truth, the gospel of your salvation, and believed in him, were sealed with the promised Holy Spirit, who is the guarantee of our inheritance until we acquire possession of it, to the praise of his glory" (Eph 1:11–14).

In The Trenches

1. What is our inheritance in Christ?

2. How should we live now in the light of such an inheritance?

Day 5

Heart Check

"Jesus said to her, 'I am the resurrection and the life. Whoever believes in me, though he die, yet shall he live, and everyone who lives and believes in me shall never die. Do you believe this?'" (John 11:25–26)

Victory

"I will restore to you the years that the swarming locust has eaten" (Joel 2:25).

Week 33—Opposite Day

Day 1

Fighting On

We carry these impediments,
These scars of imperfection,
All our lives.

They rise like slivers,
Sharply wedged beneath thin skin,
To prick our pride,
Intruding,
Painfully uprooting
parts we thought had died,
Or surely conquered.
Why are we still in the battle here?

Our flaws keep bubbling up.
And we are often
Unprepared
Because we look inside instead of up.
Forgetting we are not the weak and wounded,
Bleeding,
Dying here,
Alone amidst a raging war.
We are the weak and wounded lifted up.
We are afflicted, but not crushed,

Struck down but not destroyed.

In suffering,

Enduring

For the sake of Christ.

We are His army,

We, His rising tide against the dark.

And we are being changed,

Transformed,

Remade,

Re-named.

And all our scars

Are fresh reminders of His work—

His mending, healing hand

creating glorious hearts from parts once base.

And all our flaws are meant to draw us

closer to the King and to His Cross,

Where even our impediments

Shout heaven's grace.

In The Trenches

1. We are coming to the end of our study. What does it mean to be a part of God's army?

2. Is it difficult to fight dragons? Is it worth it?

Day 2

Studying the Battle Plan

Read Philippians 2:5-11. Re-acquaint yourself with these verses. We have referred to them earlier in our study.

> "After this I looked, and behold, a great multitude that no one could number, from every nation, from all tribes and peoples and languages, standing before the throne and before the Lamb, clothed in white robes, with palm branches in their hands, and crying out with a loud voice, 'Salvation belongs to our God who sits on the

throne, and to the Lamb!' And all the angels were standing around the throne and around the elders and the four living creatures, and they fell on their faces before the throne and worshiped God, saying, 'Amen! Blessing and glory and wisdom and thanksgiving and honor and power and might be to our God forever and ever! Amen'" (Rev 7:9–12).

In The Trenches

1. Who is the central focus of both of these passages?
2. How does the second passage fulfill and complete the first?

Day 3

Scouting the Territory

We started with a wedding; a holy alliance between God and man, and between a man and his bride. Man broke the alliance. He declared war on God, and discovered in the process that he had declared war on himself. Like the great myths of old, the man and his bride had awakened dragons they could not control. Only God himself could clean up this mess, and how do you broker a truce with the one you have betrayed? How can anything be made right when you begin to realize that you, too, have become one of the dragons?

Dragon slaying is a holy quest requiring a holy God. It is the ultimate quest; demanding perfect wisdom, perfect obedience, perfect love, and perfect sacrifice. From Adam on, we have proven over and over that we cannot complete this quest. In fact, we are miserable failures. We will always be better at being dragons than vanquishing them. But the Slayer is everything we can never be. And out of his compassion he chose to be our champion. The Slayer chose the hard road. He *chose* the dirty, messy road; the road of pain and blood; the road of loving sacrifice that leads to death. Only this road overcomes pride and self. Only holy blood by a willing and perfect sacrifice can scrub the dragon from our hearts. It is what my grandson would call, "Opposite Day," when everything we thought was true, is actually only true upside down. On Opposite Day, trials develop strength, and weakness makes what is broken whole.

The Dragon loves pride. The Slayer chose humiliation. The Dragon loves status, position, and power. The Slayer chose shame. The Dragon loves self. The Slayer chose us—you and me. The Dragon loves to accuse. The Slayer identified himself with us: the betrayers, the liars, the rebels, the ungrateful enemy, and became the accused. Who would have thought; with power, with pride and anger heating the center of our hearts, that the Slayer would take on himself the terrible fire and brimstone intended for us? And that his willingly laying down his life for the ones who betrayed and hated him the most, would finally and decisively tear away The Dragon's deadly grip, would free us to live and love at last, would save us from ourselves?

Then the Slayer wooed us. He named us his beloved, his bride. He chose a new and greater alliance, an eternal alliance between the Man/God and his bride that cannot be broken. And from this alliance will come a new wedding in a new heaven and earth, where there will be no more dragons, no more mourning, and no more death. "Behold," he will say on that wedding day, his glorious, never-ending Opposite Day, "I am making all things new. What was unholy I have made holy. There will be no more dragons." To us, and to the first bride and groom, who have waited patiently over the millennia for this glorious moment, it will be the grandest Opposite Day of all.

In The Trenches

1. What makes Opposite Day so unexpected and so powerful?

2. What amazes you the most about God's love and sacrifice?

Day 4

Vincit

You think that wickedness will win?
You don't know Grace, or Justice's place.
For evil hearts will play their parts,
They are just players on a stage
of their design,
And every rage and terror
they display,

Are only echoes,
Shadows of defeated wars,
Hollow acting,
Driving,
Seething hard
against The Reign of Righteousness already set.

They are the sin,
The appetites for death,
The love of dread,
Their pride, unlocked obsessions
Firmly wrested,
Fights dismantled,
Damned where Holy Blood was spent.

And only judging fire waits to fall,
To mete such shadows into ash.
These crooked branches,
Stubble only waiting for the flame,
Are empty lives,
Discarded destinies
of bitterness and curses
Cast for bonfires fame.

They cannot stand
before the King.
Instead,
All wickedness will crawl,
They must obey,
And bow
before the Master's Name.

Wind Down

Wind down,
Wind down old earth,
Most ancient of Creation,
Wobbling in orbit,
Out of sync.

You've borne
the blood of man
too long.

The Milky Way,
And all the stars of heaven,
Have been listening to your groaning out in space,
Your aging faces into dark,
Awaiting restoration's glorious Light and Grace.

Wind down,
Wind down old earth.
We fly around the sun with you,
In eager expectation
of the end
that is Beginning once forever.
Be forever!
Mend!

In The Trenches

1. What is the destiny of all dragons?

2. What is the destiny of this world?

3. Why are believers in eager expectation of all endings?

Day 5

Heart Check

1. Read Rev 21:3–4. It promises the end of death, the end of dragons, the end of sorrow, and the beginning of eternal fellowship where God with us takes on a whole new dimension.

2. Are you ready?

Week 34—The Un–Dragon Book

Day 1

It's Done!

The triumph of the Lamb is blood,
His sacrifice,
His blood poured out.

No need for goats,
No hope in sheep,
No daily bulls and doves,
No blood of animals suffice.
No more.

It's done!
It's done!

The list of charges read aloud
before the dock,
Have all been paid.
The violence on One
Has smashed
The rebel's grand parade
of substitutes,
And smothered pride.

No stain remains.
No need to hide.

No need to garner fig leaves.

Truth has been exposed,
Revealed at last,
And darkness cast out
into night,
Where shadows drifting,
Crumble into dust,
Are tossed
like dirt upon a grave
already emptied,
Death deserted,
Death despised,
Is now denied its power.

Life instead
is swallowed up by Light.

In The Trenches

1. How much of this poem refers to the cross and resurrection? How much could refer to the end of time and the new heavens and new earth?

2. Can you find hints of Genesis 3? Leviticus 1–6? Hebrews 9? Revelation 20:1–10, 21:22–25?

Day 2

Studying the Battle Plan

"Blessed be the LORD!
For he has heard the voice of my pleas for mercy.
The LORD is my strength and my shield;
in him my heart trusts, and I am helped;
my heart exults,
and with my song I give thanks to him.
The LORD is the strength of his people;

he is the saving refuge of his anointed.
Oh, save your people and bless your heritage!
Be their shepherd and carry them forever" (Ps 28:6–9).

In The Trenches

1. How has the Lord been your strength and shield?

2. What are your favorite hymns and why? Are they in praise of God's attributes? Thanksgiving for Christ's work on your behalf? Reminders of his faithfulness and love for you?

Day 3

The Groom Comes

He does not come to ask,
But claims His bride,
The Church betrothed to Him in blood,
His people held secure,
Protected and beloved.

"Come dearest heart,
Come to the feast prepared for us,
The wedding promised and proclaimed before the world
is now at hand,
The promises I made are now begun.

Be glad! Be free!
Come dearest heart,
Come be with me."

And Cinderella,
Rising from her ash heap,
Dons her shoes,
Her dancing slippers glistening in His light,
His grace.

Her miseries now fade,

All sad and lost forgotten
as she meets His gaze.

No longer sorrows,
No rebellions,
No more jealousies and hate—
Forgiven,
Washed,
And dressed for glory and for life,
Messiah and His bride walk through the Gate.

In The Trenches

1. This poem imagines the marriage supper of the Lamb on a personal level. You, reader, are a member of the bride of Christ, and your groom, Jesus, has come to take you to the great feast. Does this poem give you greater confidence and hope in his love for you?

2. Read Revelation 19: 1–10 and see the marriage supper of the Lamb from the viewpoint of the entire church. The church throughout time is the true bride. How do you see this great feast? Who has provided the glorious gown for the bride? How was it provided? Hint: Who made the saints righteous?

Day 4

Scouting the Territory

Have you noticed over our study that there is less and less about dragons and more and more about Christ? Wasn't this book supposed to be about dragons? Well, yes, and no. We need to remember two profound thoughts. The first is how we should understand dragons. C.S. Lewis says:

> "There are two equal and opposite errors into which our race can fall about devils. One is to disbelieve in their existence. The other is to believe, and to feel an excessive and unhealthy interest in them. They themselves are equally pleased by both errors and hail a materialist or a magician with the same delight."[1]

1. Lewis, Preface, *Screwtape Letters*, 17.

We need to recognize that dragons are real, that we are truly in a battle. But we don't want to dwell on them, or give them power.

The second thought is even more profound, and it is the central core to God's battle plan: fix your eyes on Jesus. The more you know Christ—worshipping him and living in thankfulness and obedience to him—the more dragons become impotent and invisible. They fade away in the presence of God's holy light. Psalm 139:12 says that "even the darkness is not dark to you; the night is bright as the day, for darkness is as light to you." Dragons are not God. They fade before him.

Now I understand that until Revelation 20 is fulfilled and Satan and all his dragons will be cast forever into the lake of fire, there is serious evil, and powers of darkness out there. And we are often in the battle. And I also understand that as long as we live in this world, we fight dragons in our hearts; dragons of fear, of pride, of anger, of discouragement, and of depression. We are tempted to make idols out of everything. We face illness and pain. And we all finally face death. Not death of the soul, but certainly physical death.

But I keep coming back to this eternal truth engraved on Jesus' scarred hands and feet, in the wound in his side. From before the foundation of the world, God chose us, he adopted us as sons and inheritors, through the life, death, and resurrection of his son, Jesus Christ. We have been redeemed. We are freed forever from slavery to sin and guilt (dragon favorites). Through the Holy Spirit our inheritance, our forgiveness, and our redemption are secure. They are guaranteed. Even death is "swallowed up in victory"(1 Cor 15:54b). God has already won. In Christ, we have already won, and you and I are part of his "mopping up" operation. Your life, your daily struggles, are all part of his cosmic strategy; leading us forward toward his ultimate victory. I find it helpful to remember that I am not only in the battle, but an integral part of God's sure and steady battle plan to complete his mission.

"Therefore," says the Apostle Paul, under the direction of the Holy Spirit, "be steadfast, immovable, always abounding in the work of the Lord, knowing that in the Lord your labor is not in vain" (1 Cor 15:58). Your labor is not in vain. It lasts forever. Dragons are for a season. Christ is forever. You are forever. Nothing can separate you from his love. Nothing can separate you from the day to day, hour by hour, sustaining power of Christ, and his grace. So stand tall, walk long, and trust him. Keep fighting, and keep your eyes fixed on Jesus.

Day 5

Heart Check

"For I consider that the sufferings of this present time are not worth comparing with the glory that is to be revealed to us . . . Likewise the Spirit helps us in our weakness. For we do not know what to pray for as we ought, but the Spirit himself intercedes for us with groanings too deep for words . . . And we know that for those who love God all things work together for good, for those who are called according to his purpose" (Rom 8:18, 26, 28).

1. What is your immediate response when facing frustration, pain, or trial?

2. What does Scripture say is the true perspective on your situation?

3. How can these verses lead you toward peace and hope, even in the most difficult times?

Footprints

"To him who loves us and freed us from our sins by his blood and made us a kingdom, priests to his God and Father, to him be glory and dominion forever and ever. Amen" (Rev 1:5–6).

Week 35—Come, Lord Jesus!

Day 1

Studying the Battle Plan

"Then I saw a new heaven and a new earth, for the first heaven and the first earth had passed away, and the sea was no more. And I saw the holy city, new Jerusalem, coming down out of heaven from God, prepared as a bride adorned for her husband. And I heard a loud voice from the throne saying, 'Behold, the dwelling place of God is with man. He will dwell with them, and they will be his people, and God himself will be with them as their God. He will wipe away every tear from their eyes, and death shall be no more, neither shall there be mourning, nor crying, nor pain anymore, for the former things have passed away'" (Rev 21:1–4).

Day 2

The Eighth Day

He was a curious boy,
Checking out each row of ants,
Industry in focused motion tree to tree,
Both boy and ant
in splendor,
Long admiring the harmony
that comes when God, Creator,
Whispers in each other's ear.

He was a curious man,
Observations became questions
leading into other questions,
Trying to understand the woof and warp of God's Creation,
Captivated by the bits of answers,
Teased by possibilities,
Tantalized by revelations,
When his own unwrapping
wrapped his mind in more enigmas,
Whispers of eternity.

Surprisingly,
His death
Instead became his Life,
His passion.
Curiouser and curiouser,
The Seventh Day becomes the Eighth,
Where vast,
Unbounded explorations of a better world,
A cosmic universe,
Could usher boy and man
Before the bright and endless journeys of forever,
Making all the more
discovering the infinite Creation,
That more glorious.

The man at last unpacked his heart and questions,
All his endless observations,
Every thought,
Before the feet,
Before the face of his Designer,
God,
Creator,
He who made,
And long sustained
(with sheer delight)
The Curious of His creation.

Day 3

Scouting the Territory

On July of 2015, I stood on the South Rim of the Grand Canyon. I don't believe there are words precise enough, big enough, or picturesque enough to properly describe the experience, but I will try. You cannot see all 14 miles across the canyon, so you have this marvelous sense of infinity stretched out before you in beautiful shades of red, orange, pink, beigey browns, grays, and greens; all layered in hill after amazing, craggy hill. Some edges look soft, while others are clearer, harder lines. And clouds drift in and out, casting interesting shadows. I was trying to absorb this incredible panorama of color and immense size, when my eight–year–old grandson stepped up to the same view and immediately shouted and laughed in sheer delight. I understood, grateful to hear out loud what we were both feeling; our shared joy in the face of great beauty. But there was also humbling awe. How mighty are the works of God!

And then I thought, how unlike us. All our culture's present worries and constant instructions about carbon footprints unintentionally express our true insignificance. We took the train to the South Rim (lots of fun, by the way). Small carbon footprint. No gas expended, no fumes. We dutifully and carefully disposed of our lunch trash, making sure to separate garbage from paper and plastic (separate bins provided). Small carbon footprint. We stayed on the proscribed trails and didn't pick up any of nature's souvenirs to take home. Small carbon footprint.

Now this is not a treatise in favor of trashing or marring God's creation. Nor is it an ecological commentary. We are all called to be good stewards of God's world. But while I was admiring God's giant earthly footprint, I found myself contemplating what kind of spiritual footprint I am leaving behind. At this time in Western history, biblical Christianity is being asked to maintain a small footprint. Keep your religious beliefs to yourself unless they match up with what is presently acceptable.

Yet there is God's footprint right in front of me—wild, majestic, overwhelmingly huge, and dangerously close. One misstep too close to the edge and his footprint swallows mine forever. And his earthly footprints are all over his creation. His thunder shouts and rumbles. His seas roar. Our sun is only one of his many stars. It is not the hottest, nor the largest. Yet I would be totally evaporated in the blink of an eye before I could even get "too close" because it is a raging ball of fire. My carbon footprint is almost invisible in comparison to his. Why should I be afraid to step out, to be noticed, to stand for truth? "Where can I go from your Spirit?" asks the psalmist. "Or where shall I flee from your presence? If I ascend to heaven, you are there! If I make my bed in Sheol, you are there! If I take the wings of the morning and dwell in the uttermost parts of the sea, even there your hand shall lead me and your right hand shall hold me" (Ps 139:7–10). If I stand at the edge of the Grand Canyon, you are there.

As a child of the King, I am always standing in his footprint. Like a child eagerly following in his father's steps, I will walk where his footprints lead me. I will speak truth, even if it makes my spiritual footprint stand out. Why? He made me a living being. I am eternal because he redeemed me, and through the Holy Spirit I am being changed. He has promised to someday recreate me. I am able to stand very close to this Son and not be consumed, for he is holding me by his life, his sacrifice, and his resurrection. And every dark place in my life is already filled with his marvelous light.

My two little feet stood on the edge of one of his earthly footprints, my heart quietly singing his doxology, "For you shall go out in joy and be led forth in peace; the mountains and the hills before you shall break forth into singing" (Isa 55:12). Someday even creation will be set free from its bondage to our corruption (Rom 8:21). No more trash on either earth or soul. "So shall my word be that goes out from my mouth," he says. "It shall accomplish that which I purpose, and shall succeed in the thing for which I sent it" (Isa 55:11). His word will succeed, and every time I speak his word, every time I am a witness of his word, I speak truth and light to a watching world. A world still lost in the dark, a world elevating the insignificant and ignoring the grand and glorious in its frantic, fruitless efforts to find a way out.

Why would I put the Light of the World under a basket, so no one could see? "Let your light shine before others," instructs Jesus, "so that they may see your good works and give glory to your Father who is in heaven" (Matt 5:16). I have seen his splendor spread out across my world. I am a witness of his salvation, and I have glimpsed the promise of future glories in his amazing footprint. I must speak. Here I stand, I can do no other.

Day 4

O worship the King all–glorious above,
O gratefully sing his power and his love:
our shield and defender, the Ancient of Days,
pavilioned in splendor and girded with praise.
O tell of his might and sing of his grace,
whose robe is the light, whose canopy space.
His chariots of wrath the deep thunderclouds form,
and dark is his path on the wings of the storm.
Your bountiful care what tongue can recite?
It breathes in the air; it shines in the light;
it streams from the hills; it descends to the plain;
and sweetly distills in the dew and the rain.
Frail children of dust, and feeble as frail,
in you do we trust, nor find you to fail;
Your mercies how tender, how firm to the end,
our Maker, Defender, Redeemer, and Friend!
O measureless Might! Ineffable Love!
While angels delight to hymn you above,
the humbler creation, though feeble their lays,
with true adoration shall lisp to your praise.[1]

Day 5

Heart Check

I am in the middle of a move—out of the first home, not yet in the second. I am in what C.S. Lewis's book, *The Magician's Nephew* called, The Wood Between the Worlds. Only mine is not quiet and dreamy, but chaotic and unsettling; the result of the consequences of all the last–ditch days of packing. Anyone who has packed their own stuff will tell you that in the early days, one tends to be more organized. Towards the end, a myriad of "stuff" is thrown into boxes with content titles that read, "garage mix," or "bedroom leftovers."

---

1. Grant, *Trinity Hymnal*, 2.

The downside of course, is that if you are like me, stuck in the middle between houses, you can't find what you want. I have no interest in going through box after box just to find a comb, a dress, or a blue sweater. So here I am at church on Sunday morning in black tennis shoes, white socks, a slightly wrinkled, yet clean shirt, and capris. I am sixty-two, and dressed for a picnic. I did find a pearl necklace. So now I am dressed for an upscale picnic.

I am trying not to cry. After all, God is more interested in my countenance (an excellent old-fashioned word for face and attitude), than my couture, but I am having trouble adjusting my unhappy heart for worship. But here is where standing for Christ, being in Christ, hits the road, and God is busily working on my wayward heart. I am no longer on the heights enjoying the wonders of the Grand Canyon. I am in the valley once again; the everyday place we all live out our faith. The Holy Spirit is gently reminding me to pack my pride back up and get to the business at hand. I certainly don't need pride today, so back it goes into the box. He is telling me to set my mind on worship. God doesn't care at all about my outfit. He does care about my heart. It is a choice, and he will help me get there.

P.S. It would seem the Lord is trying to tell me something. The sermon is all about disappointments, failures, and how God is still in charge, is still at work; accomplishing what he has planned all along. I may not have walked into the service with a smile, but I will leave with one. I will end by quoting what I wrote earlier: "His word will succeed, and every time I speak his word, every time I am a witness of his word, I speak truth and light to a watching world, a world still lost in the dark; a world elevating the insignificant and ignoring the grand and glorious in its frantic and fruitless efforts to find a way out." And I should add, every day it seems, his word speaks volumes just to me.

Bibliography

Airaksinen, Toni, "Smith College Hires Firm To Operate 24/7 'Bias Response' Hotline", Campusreform.org. (website), Posted October 24, 2016. Accessed October 24, 2016.

Bennett, Arthur, ed. *The Valley of Vision.* Carlisle: The Banner of Truth Trust, first printing, 1975, last reprint, 2001.

Carson, D.A. *The Gospel According To John, The Pillar New Testament Commentary.* Grand Rapids: William B. Eerdmans, 1991.

Ciampa, Laura. "Infanticide: Children As Chattel," The website for *The American Feminist®*, published by Feminists for Life of America, Volume 4, No. 4 (Winter 1999–2000 Embracing All Life), www.feministsforlife.org/taf/1999/Winter99-00.pdf.

Duguid, Iain M. *Living in The Grip of Relentless Grace, The Gospel in the lives of Isaac and Jacob.* Phillipsburg: P & R, 2002.

Gordon, Ernest. *To End All Wars.* Grand Rapids: Zondervan, 1963, 2002.

Grant, Robert, (1779–1838). *O Worship The King,* Trinity Hymnal. Atlanta: Great Commission, 1990.

Kentucky National Guard. (website). *History of The Guard, Kentuckians in Action.* "From a Time of Peace To a Time of Brother Against Brother, 1825–1874", http://kynghistory.ky.gov/Our-History/History-of-the-Guard/Pages/default.aspx, accessed April 17, 2015.

Lewis, C. S. *The Great Divorce, Preface.* London: C.S. Lewis Pte. Ltd., 1946, Copyright renewed, 1973.

———. *The Magician'S Nephew.* C.S. Lewis Pte. Ltd., 1955.

———. *Mere Christianity.* C.S. Lewis. Pte. Ltd., 1942, 1943, 1944, 1952.

———. *The Silver Chair.* C.S. Lewis. Pte. Ltd., 1953.

———. *The Screwtape Letters.* C.S. Lewis Pte. Ltd., 1942.

———. *The Voyage of The Dawn Treader.* C.S. Lewis Pte. Ltd., 1952.

———. *The Weight of Glory.* C.S. Lewis Pte. Ltd., 1949.

Luther, Martin, (1483–1546). Translated by Frederick H. Hedge, 1805–1890. *A Mighty Fortress,* Trinity Hymnal. Atlanta: Great Commission, 1990.

Owens, Tiffany. "Walking Through Fire." *World Magazine* (www.wng.org), March 8, 2014.

Raffel, Burton. Printed excerpts from Beowulf translated by Burton Raffel, translation copyright© 1963 by Burton Raffel, renewed 1991 by Burton Raffel. Used by permission of New American Library, an imprint of Penguin Publishing Group, a division of Penguin Random House LLC. All rights reserved.

Electronic version excerpts from Beowulf reprinted by permission of Russell & Volkening as agents for the author. Copyright © 1962 Burton Raffel, renewed in 1991 by Burton Raffel.

Rodigast, Samuel, (1649-1708). Translated by Catherine Winkworth (1863. Alt. 1961). *Whate'er My God Ordains is Right*. Trinity Hymnal, Atlanta: Great Commission, 1990.

Sailhamer, John H. *The Expositor's Bible Commentary, Revised Edition, Volume 1, Genesis – Leviticus*, edited by Tremper Longman III and David E. Garland. Grand Rapids: Zondervan, 2008.

Sayers, Dorothy. *Letters to a Diminished Church*. Nashville: Thomas Nelson, Inc, 2004.

Ten Boom, Corrie and Elizabeth and John Sherrill. *The Hiding Place*. Grand Rapids: Chosen Books, A division of Baker Publishing Group, 1971 and 1984 by Corrie ten Boom, and 2006 by Elizabeth and John Sherrill.

Tripp, Paul David. Preface to *Home: How Heaven And The New Earth Satisfy Our Deepest Longings*, by Elyse Fitzpatrick. Minneapolis: Bethany House, 2016.

———. *A Quest For More, Living For Something Bigger Than You*. Greensboro: New Growth, 2007.

Ulatowski, Leah. "He's Made Us Richer," Sheyboygan Press, January 3, 2016. Gannett-Community.

Waltke, Bruce K. *The Book of Proverbs, Chapters 15–31, The New International Commentary on The Old Testament*. Grand Rapids: William B. Eerdmans, 2005.

Watlke, Bruce K., and Cathi J. Fredericks. *Genesis: A Commentary*. Grand Rapids: Zondervan, 2001.

Wasson, Jae. "Sowing Fear: Why Are Isis–Affiliated Groups Putting Random Americans on Hit Lists?" *World Magazine* (www.wng.org), October 15, 2016.

Welch, Edward T. *Depression, Looking Up From The Stubborn Darkness*. Greensboro: New Growth, 2011.

———. *Running Scared*. Greensboro: New Growth, 2007.

———. *Side By Side*. Wheaton: Crossway, 2015.

ESV study notes, 1 Samuel 17:4–11; Joshua 24:1; Malachi 2: 13–14; John 4:5, taken from the *ESV® Study Bible* (*The Holy Bible, English Standard Version®*), Wheaton: Crossway Bibles, a Publishing ministry of Good News, 2008).